Living with a Brother or Sister with Special Needs

A Book for Sibs

by

DONALD J. MEYER

PATRICIA F. VADASY

REBECCA R. FEWELL

With a Foreword by Thomas H. Powell

Drawings by R. Scott Vance

UNIVERSITY OF WASHINGTON PRESS

Seattle and London

Library of Congress Cataloging in Publication Data

Meyer, Donald J.
  Living with a brother or sister with special needs.

  Includes bibliographies and index.
    1. Handicapped children—Family relationships—Addresses, essays, lectures. 2. Handicapped children—Home care—Addresses, essays, lectures. 3. Brothers and sisters—Addresses, essays, lectures. I. Vadasy, Patricia F. II. Fewell, Rebecca R. III. title
  [DNLM: 1. Handicapped. 2. Mental Retardation.
  3. Sibling Relations. WS 105.5.F2 M612L]
  HV888.M49   1985   362.4′088054   85-40356
  ISBN 0-295-96287-9
  ISBN 0-295-96272-0 (pbk.)

Contents

Note to Siblings

We have a friend, Paul, who's twelve years old. Paul is like a lot of junior high students. He likes to play soccer and video games with his friends. Sometimes they go out for ice cream after school, or listen to records and talk. But there's something Paul doesn't talk about with his friends. He has a six-year-old sister, Barbara, who is deaf and mentally retarded. Some days Paul would like to tell his friends how proud he is of Barbara when she learns something new—like how to make the sign for dog, or how to eat without making a huge mess. Other days he'd like to tell them how angry he is at Barbara. But Paul doesn't talk about Barbara to his friends. They wouldn't really understand.

There are thousands of children like Paul who have a brother or sister with a handicap. But Paul is luckier than most of them, because there is someone he can talk to about Barbara, and someone who can answer his questions. Paul comes to the programs we offer every few months for siblings (brothers and sisters) of handicapped children. It's not like school, although we do learn about things—like what it means to be mentally retarded. But we mostly talk about things that siblings don't get a chance to discuss with their parents or their friends—like what to do when you get angry at your special sib, or how to tell your parents you don't want to take your special sib with you to the shopping mall. We talk about feelings that sibs like Paul can't really explain to people who don't have a handicapped brother or sister. And we also have fun together. We have barbecues, or we make pasta, or we learn to juggle. And we make new friends.

Sibs like Paul who come to programs for sibs probably don't feel as lonely as they used to feel. They also have answers to some of the questions they had about their brother's or sister's handicap, or what will happen to their special sib when he or she grows up.

We wish that there were special programs for siblings all over the country. But right now there aren't. We'd like sibs everywhere to be able to talk about their feelings with other sibs who understand. We'd like other sibs to know that they aren't the only ones who feel embarrassed or guilty sometimes about their brother or sister. We'd also like to be able to answer the questions that sibs have so that they understand more about their brother's or sister's handicap and can explain it to other people, like their friends, who ask them questions about it.

That's the reason we wrote this book. We couldn't write about every handicap, but we tried to write about the most common ones, and to answer the questions that siblings most often asked us. The siblings in our programs told us a lot about the feelings they have about their special brother or sister. They were often surprised to find that the other siblings felt the same way. We wrote about these special feelings, because we think it helps to know that you aren't the only one who feels the way you do.

We wrote this book for siblings. Because you are a sibling, you are the only one who can tell us if the book helps you. We'd like to know if we answered any of your questions about your sib's handicap, or if we wrote about feelings that you've had. To make it possible for you to tell us these things, we have included some questions at the end of this book. We would appreciate it if you would take time to answer the questions after you have used the book. If this is a library book, don't write on the page, but write down your answers on a separate sheet of paper and send it to us. You don't have to include your name and address unless you want us to answer a question you have. We'll read all your comments and use them to help make this the best book possible for sibs of children with special needs.

"Why did it happen?"

"When did he get handicapped?"

"Will she have to wear those thick glasses all her life?"

"What does Down syndrome mean?"

"Why did one twin get it and not the other?"

"Will he learn to write and do math quickly?"

"Will she be able to take care of herself?"

"What happens if mom and dad die?"

When we talked to brothers and sisters of children with handicaps, those were some of the questions they had about their siblings. We listened to these questions and used them to plan the workshops we offer for groups of young siblings. These meetings give siblings a chance to get information about handicaps and issues surrounding the handicap. They also give sibs a chance to find the answers to questions they may not have felt comfortable asking their parents. Perhaps most important, the meetings are an opportunity for siblings to meet other sibs—which many have never done before—and discover that other children have the same kinds of questions and feelings that they do.

When we first met with siblings and asked them to tell us what caused their brother's or sister's handicap, we found that they often had basic questions and misunderstandings. Some of the siblings wrote:

"I don't really know what caused it."
"I think it was mom's stomach."
"It was the amount of cromozomes."
"A piece of steel fell on mom's leg when she was pregnant."
"It was childbirth."
"It was too much excitement."
"The bag broke."

Siblings often clung to unconnected bits of information they had been given about their sibling's handicap, so that their understanding was fragmentary or possessed a magical significance. The workshops offered us an excellent opportunity to give siblings the facts they needed to answer some of their questions and to clear up the confusion that often came to light when they tried to explain their sibling's problems.

Siblings also shared with us problems they experienced as a result of having a brother or sister with a handicap.

"Friends make fun of her."
"He bites me."
"She embarrasses me when she sucks on her hand in front of my friends."
"If kids make fun of her I tell them to stop or I'll sock them."
"Sometimes I cry without knowing why."
"When he screams it scares me."
"I get embarrassed when strangers stare and think she's dumb."
"It's hardest when people laugh and she doesn't know what she's doing wrong."
"Mom needs to spend a lot more time with him than with me."

The small group discussions and social activities we organized in the workshops encouraged the children to share these common problems and, more important, their individual ways of solving them. This way a sibling benefited not only from knowing that other sibs face similar problems but also from learning that there are many ways to solve a problem. When appropriate, we would supplement their solutions by suggesting specific strategies siblings can use to respond to friends who say thoughtless or mean things about their handicapped brother or sister. We also discussed behavior modification techniques that can be used to discourage the child with special problems from pestering a brother or sister when friends are visiting.

We learned a lot from the children who came to our sibling workshops. We learned by talking to them in small discussion groups and by listening to them in the group sessions and during social activities, such as the cookout or the pasta-making session we organized.

At the end of our workshops, we would ask ourselves how we could share with other siblings what we had learned. The siblings at our meetings pointed out two major areas of need: the need for simple, clear explanations about the causes and nature of handicaps, and the need for reassurance and support for their feelings about their sib who has special needs. The siblings also shared their insights on solving problems that siblings commonly face. The informal setting of our meetings with siblings helped us to respond directly to these children's concerns and to share the information they needed. What better way could we reach young siblings in other parts of the country—siblings who don't have access to groups like ours—than to write down, in plain language, what we learned and what we shared with the children in our workshops?

That is how we got the idea for this book. Books have some advantages that sibling groups don't have. A book can reach more siblings than we could ever talk to individually, and we can provide detailed information on more handicaps and issues in a book than we can in a workshop. Children can also use the information in a book whenever they feel like it, and go back to it again and again.

Before writing this book, we talked to even more siblings, and read more books about handicaps, and talked to doctors and nurses and teachers. And we tried to put together all that we had learned. In preparing the book we wanted to make it as easy as possible for a young sibling to find an answer to a particular question. We hope that readers will use the table of contents and the index when they are in a hurry to find an answer to a question. We also hope that readers will have some time to just sit down and read longer parts of the book—especially the first chapter, because it deals with feelings that many siblings have in common, and the last two chapters, because most children with handicaps will receive the special services described in Chapter

8, and because all families have to make some kind of plans for the future described in the the last chapter.

Only our readers can tell us if we have done what we set out to do—help other siblings. That is why we have included a page at the end of the book that we would like readers to fill out (or if this is a library book, the questions should be answered on another sheet of paper) and return to us. These comments will help us do a better job of writing for siblings, and in making changes in the book so that it will be more useful to them. We hope that our book will help readers share the feelings of one sibling, who told a workshop group that the best thing about having a sister with a handicap is "she's special, and not like anyone else."

Foreword

Just last week Cate was born. She came into the world in the usual way, surrounded by joyful parents, brothers, grandparents, and friends. Like all newborns, she is the source of hopes and expectations to her family and friends. Most importantly, her parents wondered, often aloud, how she would add to the family constellation, how she would fit into and strengthen the family system. Prior to her arrival, her parents speculated about her possible relationship to her oldest brother, Nick, who happens to have autism and mental retardation. Will she understand? Will she still love him and accept him as her oldest brother? How will they interact? How will we explain Nick's disabilities in a clear, easy-to-understand manner? Her parents wondered how they would meet the challenge of meeting multiple responsibilities to this new family member, as well as to their other children, one of whom requires more time, more patience, and more parental resources. Cate's parents wondered if they would find the help they needed from other family members, friends, and the professionals that worked with their son Nick.

This past June, Michelle graduated from the eighth grade. Two weeks before the ceremony, Michelle, alone in the car with her mother, asked, "Does Timmy have to come to the graduation?" All of her friends would be there with their families. Michelle felt that they would all be staring at Timmy, who is 10 years old, does not speak, is not toilet trained, and has frequent and loud tantrums. "Why does he always have to come? Can't we get a baby sitter?" Michelle's mom was a bit taken by surprise. They were a family—a strong, close family—despite the challenges Timmy posed. After some initial debate, Michelle's parents found a babysitter. As they left for the graduation, Michelle said to her parents, "You know I love Timmy. He's my brother. It's just hard for me sometimes. Thanks for treating me special too!" Somehow, Michelle learned to talk openly and honestly with her parents. No doubt she learned this because her parents took the time to listen to her and recognize her unique needs and concerns.

For years, parents, brothers, and sisters have grappled with the task of raising children with developmental disabilities. Up until now, there has been no guide book, no Dr. Spock-like reference, no family atlas to make the journey any easier. Likewise, practitioners working with families in which one member has a disability have long recognized the need for a guide book written for brothers and sisters, which would also serve to help parents and professionals. What was needed was a book which would help siblings sort out and deal with their many and mixed feelings, like anger, joy, confusion, jealousy, fear, love, guilt, and pride. What was needed was a book that would explain disabilities in a factual, easy-to-understand manner. What was needed was a book which also presented some specific strategies to help brothers and sisters meet the unique and often intense challenges of living with a sibling with a disability.

Don Meyer, Pat Vadasy, and Rebecca Fewell, professionals with a substantial amount of understanding and sensitivity to the needs of siblings, recognized what was needed and did something about it; they wrote this book. Finally, we have a comprehensive book written especially for brothers and sisters. Finally, we have a book that deals directly with sensitive topics in a realistic manner, utilizing the experience of the many siblings with whom the authors have worked. Finally, we have a book written by individuals who have a firm grasp of the literature and scientific research, which enables presentation of complex material in a straightforward, easy-to-comprehend style.

A few characteristics of this book need special recognition. Throughout, the authors use many vignettes and quotes from siblings. I especially enjoyed the brief story of Charlie, Mike, and Tony at the special Olympics. It made me stop, think, and reconsider what siblings learn when they grow up with a disabled brother or sister.

The organization of the book reflects the notion that all siblings, no matter what disability their brother or sister has, share a number of unique concerns and needs. The first chapter, which is my favorite, deals with these real concerns and needs. "What do I tell my friends about my sister Monica?" "Why do I feel angry, sad, happy, embarrassed, and jealous?"

The authors not only discuss these concerns and needs, but also provide explanations for them in a fashion that enables siblings to understand that such concerns and needs are a normal part of their growing-up process. This chapter provides ample suggestions to siblings on strategies for dealing with friends, parents, and their own emotions and ways to interact with the disabled child.

The first chapter provides a strong foundation for the next chapters, which detail various disabilities. Meyer, Vadasy, and Fewell provide clear, concise factual information for siblings. This information will help dispel myths and misconceptions about particular disabilities, leading to a better understanding and acceptance of the disability.

The final chapters on educational services and the future bring universal sibling themes back into focus. Siblings, like their parents, need to understand human services and are often anxious about the future. Again, the emphasis here is on information sharing.

Although written especially for siblings, it would be a shame if this book were only read by brothers and sisters. It has a clear message for parents and professionals. It should be read and reread by moms and dads as well as by anyone attempting to help families. We will all learn to better help siblings after reading this book.

It seems to me that the authors wrote so well because they took the time to recognize the importance of siblings in the life of children with disabilities. They recognized the importance of siblings in the family system. Their comments and suggestions are pragmatic because they took the time to listen to siblings and understand their needs and concerns. Because they took the time, our job as parents and professionals will be much easier.

One final note, before you begin to read this book: Do not expect a heavy, "oh-woe-is-me" attitude. This book is exciting and unique because it is so positive, so up-beat. The book stresses the positive outcomes of living with a brother or sister with a disability, while recognizing the difficulties.

I expect that this book will have a significant, positive impact on the lives of families. *Living with a Brother or Sister* will serve as a standard for future works for and about siblings. I hope this book finds its way into local libraries, schools and into the hands of all sisters and brothers who are faced with the challenge of living with a sibling who has a developmental disability.

THOMAS H. POWELL, Director
Connecticut's University Affiliated Programs   July 8, 1985

Acknowledgments

So many people have helped us write this handbook for siblings that we hardly know where to begin to express our appreciation. We would first like to thank the Department of Health and Human Services for funding this project (Grant #90DD0021) under their Discretionary Funds Program, as a Project of National Significance, and thus making this book possible.

We owe our largest debt of thanks to the many siblings who provided the inspiration and encouragement for the book. We want to thank the siblings and parents who participated in the SEFAM sibling workshops, who shared their firsthand experiences as members of a handicapped child's family. The contents of this book reflect many of their concerns. We also want to thank the following siblings who took the time to read our book in manuscript form and tell us what they thought about it: Tig and Sarabeth Billyeu, Jennifer Groll, Jeff and Lesley Heath, Jennifer Liddle, Jennie Muma, Gerald, Marion, Patti, and Steven Pounds, Andrea Rytter, Stephanie Strausz, and Bessie Whittaker.

We consulted many reference sources and specialists in the areas we wrote about to be sure that all the information we present is as accurate and up to date as possible. We want to thank the following individuals, who are experts in their fields, for reading and suggesting changes and additions to the manuscript to make the book more useful to young readers: Joseph Belmonte, Dr. David Coulter, Kathy Fennell, Pam Hofer, Liz Ingman, Dr. Mitchell Kar-

ACKNOWLEDGMENTS

ton, Judy LeConte, Dr. Tom Lovitt, Dr. Richard Neel, Helen Pym, Sharon Rytter, Greg Schell, and Janine Thunder.

Our very special thanks go to Dr. Mary Cerreto and Dr. Nancy Miller, who were invaluable advisers to this project. Dr. Cerreto's work with siblings has made her sensitive to their needs, and she generously and kindly shared her special insights with us. Both Dr. Cerreto and Dr. Miller, who counsels and writes for siblings, helped us to walk the fine line of trying to furnish just what—but not more than—a young reader would want to know. We have tried to heed their advice to write with grace and clarity.

Finally, we thank Susan Isoshima, Valerie Curnow, Susan Lewis, Adrienne Peterson, and Gail Britto for their patient, meticulous preparation of this manuscript. We were most fortunate to have their dependable and experienced assistance.

Living with a Brother or Sister with Special Needs

Chapter 1

What It's Like to Have a Sibling Who Is Handicapped

You are the brother or sister of a child who has a handicap. You and your sibling (that's your brother or sister) are special people. You have feelings and problems and questions that concern your special sibling. Maybe you've thought that no one else has feelings like yours. Most likely your friends won't understand some feelings you have—feelings like being embarrassed by your special sib, or angry at a friend who says something mean about your sib. Some of these feelings are hard to talk about, because who would understand? Then there are other feelings—good feelings—that you'd like to share. Like the proud way you feel when your special sib learns to do something, and you know how much work went into it. Or the good feeling you have when a friend of yours stands up for your sibling.

Maybe you've thought that you were the only person who has had such feelings. But all siblings of children with special needs sometimes have those same feelings. Many of these feelings can help you grow and understand things about life that other people take a long time to learn.

In this chapter, we'll talk about the feelings and experiences you probably share with many other siblings. We will talk about all the kinds of feelings you have—both good and bad. We will also discuss some of the special qualities that siblings like you have—qualities that make *you* a very special person.

Friends

*"Sometimes, friends need to be reminded that behind the handicap
is a person."*

Kevin was so angry he wanted to kick something—or, better yet, someone. As he and his friends finished their basketball practice, a group of wheelchair athletes came into the gym to play basketball. Before they left, Kevin and his teammates watched the athletes roll their wheelchairs on the court and begin to play. Just as they were leaving through the gym door, one of Kevin's teammates yelled—loud enough for everyone to hear—"Hire the handicapped! They're fun to watch!" Some of the other kids laughed. Kevin, whose brother has cerebral palsy, said nothing. All that night and the next day he had a knot in his stomach.

Chen wishes people would understand that he and his sister are two different people. Chen and his twin sister, Helen, go to the same school. He is in the sixth grade and Helen is in a class for children who have special learning problems. Although Helen tries, she has a hard time reading anything harder than a book for second graders.
At recess or after school, Chen and his friends sometimes tease each other. That's usually okay, except when they call Chen a "retard" because his sister needs special help in school. He tries to ignore it because he knows that if he gets mad, his friends will tease him even more. Still, it hurts a lot.

Melissa hates to bring her girlfriends home. Kelly, her older sister, is retarded, and doesn't have any friends in the neighborhood. So whenever Melissa brings friends home to play, Kelly barges in. She always wants Melissa's friends to play with her stupid little dolls. Mostly, Melissa's friends are polite to Kelly, although a few of them will look at each other and snicker when Kelly starts up. Then Melissa gets red in the face and sometimes wishes Kelly would take a long walk and not come back.

Friends are great to have and important to all of us. But for some brothers and sisters of children with special needs, friends can be a special problem. Here are some problems sibs may have with friends:

—Friends sometimes make fun of children who are different, maybe even your brother or sister.

—Friends may tease you. They may say that because your sibling is handicapped, you must be too.

—When your friends are around, things your sibling does may embarrass you.

People who make fun of persons with handicaps usually don't know any better. They're not "stupid," but they probably have not been around someone with a handicap. People who have never had a chance to get to know someone with special needs often see only how the handicapped person is different. They may see only what the person with a handicap looks like, not what is inside. They may get nervous or even feel afraid when they are around a handicapped person. They don't know that all human beings have special qualities, including those who are handicapped. They don't realize how much the mean things they say can hurt both the person who is handicapped and the people who care for him, like Kevin.

Most sibs say they wouldn't make friends with someone who makes fun of handicapped people. But there are times when your good friends may say something mean or thoughtless about someone with a handicap. They may call the kids in the special education class "retards," or make fun of how they walk or talk. When friends do this, it can make you feel bad because you really like these friends but you love your sib too. What can you do?

First don't join in with them just to be part of the crowd. This will only make you feel guilty later (see p. 11). Let your friends know that making jokes about someone's handicap—something that a person can't change—is not fair. Often when people see a person with a handicap, all they see is the handicap. They need to be reminded that behind the handicap is a person. A good way to do this is to point out some of the person's qualities. If your friend laughs at the unusual way a child walks, you might say something like, "Yeah, but have you ever seen him smile? He's got a great laugh and he's really a neat kid."

If your friends make fun of your special sib, let them know that it makes you feel uncomfortable, sad, or angry. You might try saying, "I feel bad when you make fun of my sister. She may be handicapped, but she's my sister and I don't like it when you do that. It's not fair."

Also, if your friends tease you, like Chen's friends do, by saying that *you* must be retarded because your sib is retarded, let them know how you feel. Let them know that you and your sibling are two different people. You could tell them, "I'm not my brother. Just because he's handicapped doesn't mean I am. If he had his choice, he wouldn't be handicapped either. It bothers me when you make fun of his handicap. Please stop it. All right?"

Most friends will stop when you tell them. They may not realize that the teasing bothers you. That's why it's important to tell them. *How* you tell them is also important. For example, you are likely to be more successful if you talk to your friend when you are alone together and not in front of other kids. Tell your friend how your feel in a way that makes it clear that you care about his or her friendship. This is a better way of talking it over than getting upset at your friend when you are in a group. But, if friends who are thoughtless don't stop after you tell them how their words and actions make you feel, you might want to look for new friends.

Sibs often ask us what they should do when they want to invite a new friend or a date home. They may worry about what their friends will think of their handicapped brother or sister. Nonhandicapped sibs may be embarrassed (see p. 16) by how their sib looks or acts. One very good way to deal with this problem is to explain your sib's handicap *before* your friend comes to your home. This makes it easier for both of you when your friend meets your special sib. Remember to tell your friend about your sib's good points. Here's how one sib told a friend about her sister who is handicapped: "Just so you won't be surprised, there is one thing you should know before you come over on Saturday. My sister Janet has cerebral palsy. She had some problems when she was born that hurt some parts of her brain. She uses a wheelchair and can't talk, but she can understand what people say to her. She has a great sense of humor and real pretty hair." A few words can go a long way to making you and your friend feel at ease. Anyway, chances are that you will notice your sibling's looks and behavior more than your friends will.

Finally, some sibs have problems with their brothers and sisters—special or not—hanging around when friends come over. Your sib may want to join in what you are doing, or may pester you or your friends for attention, like Kelly does to Melissa. If your sib bothers you in order to get attention, try ignoring her. Read the section on "Behavior Problems" (p. 47) for ideas about how to ignore a sibling effectively. If this doesn't work, consider going to your room or to a part of the house where your sib is not allowed to go. You may have to get your parents to help out.

If you don't want your sib to hang around when your friends are visiting, you may need to let your sib and your parents know—in a calm way. This doesn't mean that you won't want to include your sib in activities at other times, but for now you would like to visit with your friends alone. If your sib has trouble understanding or accepting your explanation, try promising some special time together later. This may satisfy your sib so you can be alone with your friends. But be sure to keep your promise.

Unselfishness

"Unselfish people give without expecting anything in return."

Even though she's severely retarded and can't see, Bonita's a lucky little girl. She has an older brother, Jerome, who's crazy about her. He puts her in her stroller and takes her out for walks and sometimes sings her songs, which make her smile and laugh. More than once, he's even changed her dirty diapers. Still, some of Jerome's friends wonder why he spends time helping a sister who can't see or walk or play games. One of his friends actually asked him why he did it. Jerome replied, "Because I know if I was retarded and Bonita *wasn't*, she'd do the same thing for me."

Unselfishness is caring about another person and not expecting to get something back from them. Many brothers and sisters of handicapped people like Jerome are unselfish. They do things for their sibs who are handicapped even though they know their brothers and sisters can't give back in the same way. Unselfish people care about other people, even those who aren't good-looking, popular, or smart. Someone once said that the best way to judge a person is to see how he treats someone who can't do anything for him or to him. An unselfish person sees what is good in each person even if a person has a handicap.

Anger

"It's okay to get angry—even at a handicapped sib. But what is important is how you get rid of those angry feelings."

For over a week, Sarah had worked on a seven-page report for school on the history of her state. On Sunday night, after she finished the report, her brother Mike, who is mentally retarded, decided to "color" her report with a crayon. Sarah caught him and got very angry. She screamed at Mike, "Don't *ever* touch my homework again!" Mike didn't understand why Sarah was yelling at him and he began to cry. That made Sarah feel bad. She wanted to teach Mike a lesson, because she had put a lot of work into her report. She was disappointed and discouraged when Mike wrecked it.

Anger is a strong feeling we have when someone mistreats or hurts us, like when your sister punches you or your brother borrows your comic books without asking. Siblings often get mad at each other. It's okay to get angry—

Sarah screamed at her brother, "Don't you ever touch my homework again!"

even at a handicapped brother or sister. After all, anger is part of life. It's also okay to get rid of those angry feelings that build up inside. But there are good and bad ways of releasing those feelings. It's better to release them so that the person understands why you are angry than to yell and make the person feel scared or hurt. What is important is *how* you get rid of those feelings.

When people express their anger, they sometimes say that they are "letting off steam." In many ways, anger is like the steam that operates a steam engine. A steam engine uses pressurized steam, as energy, to turn the engine. Anger, used correctly, can be a kind of "energy" that lets people know how you feel and why you are upset, so they can change the way they behave.

But anger, like steam, can hurt people if not used correctly. Just as the steam that is released from an engine can burn someone who gets too near to it, anger can hurt someone if it is released all at once or in a thoughtless way.

Most of us can remember a time when someone was extremely angry with us because of something we did. Their anger may have been so great that they were mean to us, or frightened us.

Holding in anger doesn't help. A steam engine that never released its steam would eventually explode. But how do you let out anger so it helps instead of hurts?

One good way is to talk about your anger using "I-statements." I-statements let others know how you feel and why you feel that way. An I-statement begins with the word "I" and goes on to describe how you feel and what makes you feel that way.

In our example, Sarah screamed at her brother, "Don't you ever touch my homework again!" If she had used an I-statement, Sarah might have said firmly, but without screaming:

"I am really angry that you scribbled on my report!"
("I" + how you feel + what makes you feel that way)

I-statements are very clear when used correctly. They are especially valuable when you want to let your special sib (who may need clear instructions) know exactly why you are angry. The better your sib understands why you are angry, the easier it will be for him or her to behave differently.

I-statements are also a safe way to blow off steam, because they don't say anything bad about the person, they only talk about what the person *did*. There is no room in an I-statement to call someone a "bad boy," a "jerk," or an "idiot."

Below are examples of angry statements that aren't clear and probably would hurt more than help. Underneath each angry statement is an I-statement that would be a better way of expressing your anger.

Angry statement:	"Cut it out, pea-brain."
I-statement:	"I don't like to be tickled when I'm trying to watch TV."
Angry statement:	"Stay out of my closet, you slob!"
I-statement:	"I really get upset when my clothes are borrowed without my permission!"
Angry statement:	"Turn that down! Now!"
I-statement:	"It hurts my ears when the radio is turned up so loud!"
Angry statement:	"Get out of here and don't come back!"
I-statement:	"I don't like to be bothered when I'm trying to visit with my friends."
Angry statement:	"I don't want to ever see you near my records again!"
I-statement:	(Try this one on your own!)

Remember the formula for an I-statement: "I" + how you feel + what makes you feel that way. When you need to let your sib or anyone else know you are angry, think about what your sib or that person has done to make you angry. Then, put together the I-statement that will let the other person know most clearly why you are angry.

Accepting Differences

"Accepting differences is something that siblings of children with special needs learn when they are still growing up."

When Robin and her friends returned to school last year, there were a lot of changes. Not only were there two classes for kids who are handicapped, but there were five new Vietnamese students. Two of those students were in Robin's class. Nobody knew how to act around the new Vietnamese students, and hardly anyone talked to them, because they couldn't speak English very well. One day at recess, Robin's friend Anne said, "I don't know what's happening to our school. First we have these weirdos in the special classes, and now we have these foreign kids. Look at the clothes they wear! School's just not the same."

Robin was surprised at what Anne had said. Robin's oldest brother Bill has Down syndrome. When he was younger and was going to school, he had to take a bus to a school that was far away from everyone else. Robin liked the idea of all kinds of kids going to school together now. Also, she thought the Vietnamese kids made school more interesting. There were already white, black, and American Indian kids at school, so why not Vietnamese kids? In a funny way, it made the school feel like a little United Nations.

Some people won't have anything to do with people who are different. Some people won't accept a person who is a different color, race, or religion, or who differs from them in other ways. They are intolerant. This means that they can't accept other people's differences. You often find that the intolerant person doesn't know much about those people. People are often intolerant of others because they have never been around someone of a different race or religion. They don't really understand how much they are like someone whose race is different, and how little they differ.

One thing that you have probably noticed if you have a special sib is how quickly some people leave your sib out of activities and conversations because he or she has a handicap. You may have classmates like Anne who won't play with the kids in the special class, even though they don't really know any of the kids. If they took the time to get to know a classmate who was blind or deaf or retarded, they might find that they had a lot in common with the handicapped classmate, even though there would be things that the classmate could not do. They would probably be surprised to find that the special classmate liked to play the same video games, or enjoyed the same music, or played the same sports that they do. They would probably be quite surprised, in fact, to discover how much the handicapped person *can* do, and that there are even some things the handicapped person can do better than they can.

Some people take a long time to learn tolerance—which means to accept that people are different. Tolerance is something that siblings of special children like Robin learn when they are still growing up. Your experiences with your special sib can help you understand that even people who are handicapped or who are different from you in some other way have a lot to offer. They can even make good friends, if you take the time to get to know them. People like Anne who don't take the time to get to know people who are different from her may never find that out.

Some brothers and sisters have a hard time accepting their sibling's handicap. It may bother them so much that their sib is different that they dislike or avoid their sibling. If you ever feel like this, you should talk to your parents or to a trusted relative or friend. You could also ask your teacher or parents if you could talk to a counselor to help you understand your feelings.

Guilt

"Guilt is what we feel when we blame ourselves for doing something we think is wrong."

"Supper's almost ready," Joel's mother announced as he was watching TV. "Will you go down the block and tell Benjamin it's time to come home?" Humph, thought Joel as he left the house, why do I always have to go get that kid in the middle of my favorite TV show?

"Benjamin!" Joel yelled impatiently as he walked down the block. Joel thought about how his brother, who is mentally retarded, was always screwing up his life. "Benjamin! It's time for supper!" He continued yelling for Benjamin all the way down the block until he reached the corner where Benjamin was playing kickball with kids younger than he was.

"Benjamin, you idiot!" Joel roared. "Didn't you hear me calling you? Boy are you stupid!"

Benjamin looked down at the ground and his lower lip began to tremble. He was about to cry. Walking home, both boys were quiet.

Benjamin was upset that his brother had yelled at him. Joel felt rotten because he had called his little retarded brother a stupid idiot. Benjamin didn't need to be reminded that he was slow. He knew that.

> "Dear diary," wrote Vanessa, "I have a terrible secret that I have never shared with anyone. Before my brother Christopher was born, I was the youngest in our family. You might say I got *a lot* of attention from my folks and my brothers and sisters. When I was four, my mom told me we were going to have a new baby in the family. I wasn't too happy about that news. Just before Christopher was born, I had what I guess you'd call a 'temper tantrum' and my mom got real upset at me. Two days later my mom had Christopher. I remember that he couldn't come home from the hospital right away because something was wrong. Chris is now eight years old. He acts very strange, can't read, and the few words he can say usually don't make sense. Dear diary, my terrible secret is that I think Chris's problems are all my fault."

Guilt is a terrible feeling. We feel it when we blame ourselves for doing something we think is wrong. Sometimes guilt is useful, and sometimes it's useless.

Useful guilt is feeling bad about a situation that you helped cause. It is the feeling you may have after you say something mean about one of your classmates; or you get angry and hit your special sib for drawing in your books; or you pretend you don't know your handicapped sib when you are out shopping.

Although useful guilt is painful, as Joel knows, it can help you. It can help you see how you can change for the better. It can help you act in ways that are kinder in order to avoid the guilty feelings you suffer later.

If you feel guilty and think about how you acted (by listening to your feelings), you may decide:

—Saying mean things about your classmate was not very kind. You may decide that he didn't deserve those mean words, and that you wouldn't like someone talking about you that way. You probably won't want to act that way again.

—It was unfair to hit your handicapped sister for drawing in your book. It was okay to get angry at her (see "Anger," p. 7), but hitting didn't help at all. She cried, you felt bad, and she *still* didn't learn not to draw in your books.

—You don't need to pretend you don't know your handicapped brother when you are out shopping. After thinking about it, you may decide that you are proud of your brother's accomplishments even though he is handicapped, and you want to let others know that you are proud of him. Of course, if he is having behavior problems at the store, ignoring him *may* be the best way to stop the problem. For some tips on ignoring, see the section on Behavior Problems on page 49.

Useless guilt is feeling bad about a situation, or the way things are, even though you didn't make them that way. You may feel this kind of guilt when you win first prize in a poster contest and you know that your friend also worked very hard and wanted to win; or you think about your good health or grades and then think about all your sibling's problems (you may wonder why you were lucky and he wasn't); or you blame yourself, like Vanessa did, for your sister's handicap because you got your mom mad and upset when she was pregnant with your sister.

Feeling guilty about these things is useless because, if you think about it, they are not your fault. You did not help cause the situation that makes you feel guilty:

—Both you and your friend did your best on the poster contest, but you won. In a spelling or a baking contest she might win, even though both of you would try very hard. Good friends wouldn't want you to feel guilty for winning. They might be disappointed they lost, but they would also be happy for you.

—You may be able to do many more things than your sib can, but this is not a good reason to feel guilty. Remember, just as you want him to do the best he possibly can, he wants you to do the best you possibly can.

—There may be many reasons why your special sib is handicapped. Some of those reasons may still be a mystery to the doctors and your parents. But none of those reasons are your fault. Upsetting your mother when she was pregnant, or playing rough with your baby sister, did not cause her to become handicapped. Her handicap was probably caused by something that no one could control or prevent.

When you feel guilty, ask yourself these questions: Is the guilt useful (do you feel bad because you helped cause the situation, like Joel did)? Or is it useless (do you feel bad, like Vanessa, even though you didn't cause the situation)? If it's useful guilt, it can help you act in a way that is better for others and yourself. It can teach you to be caring. If it's useless guilt, get rid of it. It's an emotion that hurts for no good reason. Don't let it waste your time or take your attention from more important things. If you just can't help feeling bad, even when you haven't caused the situation, try talking about your feelings with your parents, teacher, school counselor, or a friend.

Jealousy

"Sometimes you probably feel like saying 'Hey, you have other kids in this family too!'"

I know this sounds crazy, Emma thought to herself, but sometimes I wish *I* had cerebral palsy! Lately Emma has been feeling jealous of her sister, Amy, who has cerebral palsy. It seems to Emma that Amy gets all the attention. Emma's soccer games never seem as important to her mother as meetings at Amy's school or at the Cerebral Palsy Center. If Emma brings home a paper with a B grade, her mother says, "Well, you'll have to try harder next time," although she makes a big fuss about anything Amy brings home, no matter how sloppy it is. When Amy was the state cerebral palsy poster child, Emma stayed with her aunt while Amy got to meet the governor at the TV station. It's just not fair, Emma thought.

If you have a special sib, chances are that sometimes you feel neglected. You feel ignored by your parents. It may seem that they don't notice you unless you do something wrong or get into trouble. They may spend so much of their time on your special sib that you feel left out, as though you're not very important. Sometimes you probably feel like saying, "Hey, you have other kids in this family too!" You want to let your parents know your sib isn't the *only* person in the family. There may even be times you wish you had a handicap like Emma so that you would get as much attention as your sib.

Parents usually have to spend more time with a special sib than with the other children in the family. The special sib often needs medical care or help to do things that you can do for yourself. Some special sibs need lots and lots of attention, while others need extra help only in certain areas. But just because your sib needs extra attention doesn't mean that you don't need some attention too. You still need to spend some time with your parents, talking about your problems and doing the things that your friends do with their parents. You need to spend an afternoon at the movies together, or go out for ice cream, or go to the swimming pool. When parents have a special child, it is easy for them to forget sometimes that all of their children need some of their time and attention.

If you feel that your parents are ignoring you, like Emma feels, try telling them just how you feel. If it's hard for you to tell your parents how you feel, try practicing with a good friend, or even in front of a mirror. Tell them you understand that your special sib needs a lot of their time. But let them know

14

that there are times when you need their help too. And there are times when you just need to spend some special moments with them, and enjoy things you like to do together. Be sure to let them know how good it feels when they let you know that they are there when you really need them.

Overinvolvement

"A family member who is overinvolved puts too much time and energy into caring for the handicapped child."

To most adults, Marty probably sounds like a perfect son and brother. Every day after school, he comes straight home and takes care of his brother Paul, who has spina bifida, so his mom can go shopping and run errands. Marty will play games with Paul, fix him a snack, take him for a walk, help him with his schoolwork, or even give him a bath. But while Marty is doing all these things, there are a lot of things he *isn't* doing. Marty isn't in the school play, he isn't playing football, he isn't hanging out with his friends, he isn't learning to play the guitar, he isn't reading books. Marty, you might say, is overinvolved with his brother Paul.

To be overinvolved means to be too close to something or someone. An overinvolved family member is one like Marty who is too close to the child with special needs. At first glance, that may not sound like a problem. After all, you and your parents want to do everything you possibly can to help your special sibling. A family member who is overinvolved, however, puts *too much* time and energy into caring for and doing things for the child with the handicap. The overinvolved person neglects his own life.

Overinvolvement can hurt all family members. The overinvolved person may not have any energy or time left for other people and other interests. Overinvolvement also leads to "burnout"—running out of energy and new ideas. Burnout hurts the handicapped child, because when the overinvolved family member runs out of energy, the child with special needs no longer gets the special care and attention that person used to give.

How can you prevent being overinvolved? Family members can do this by reminding themselves that everyone in the family has needs, not just the handicapped child. For example, you need to make friends, practice basketball or soccer, and spend time with your parents. Family members need to spend time with each other and pay attention to each other, even if there is a handicapped child in the family. All family members may have to give up some of the time and attention they would get if the child weren't handicapped, but no one in the family should give up so much that he or she stops growing as a person.

Understanding

"It takes time to understand how hard it is for someone with a handicap to do things most people don't even think about. But you understand."

Margaret was sitting with her classmates at a school baseball game. Everyone was watching the member on the opposite team who was getting ready to bat. He walked to home plate with a severe, uneven limp. It looked as though he either had cerebral palsy or had been in an accident. At his side was another boy who would run the bases for him. Margaret admired his courage for getting up there and showing everyone what he *could* do. It reminded her of her brother Tom, who has cystic fibrosis. Even though it is often difficult, Tom always tries to do his best at whatever he does. Secretly, Margaret hoped that the batter would knock the ball out of the park and score a home run, even though he was from another school.

There is an old American Indian saying, "Do not judge a man until you have walked 20 miles in his moccasins." This saying explains a lot about understanding—sharing another person's emotions and knowing how that person feels. Siblings of people with special needs, like Margaret, are often understanding of people who are different or who are not as lucky as others. Because these siblings have grown up with someone who has a handicap, they appreciate the big and little everyday challenges and difficulties that people with handicaps experience.

Embarrassment

"Sometimes you just want to pretend you don't know your special sib."

Only an hour ago Michelle couldn't wait to go shopping for school clothes at the mall. Then her mother told her that her sister Jenny, who is handicapped, would be coming too. Now she dreaded the idea.

This is just what I need, thought Michelle to herself. She had just started junior high. What would happen if the kids from her new school saw her at the mall with Jenny? And that awful wheelchair? And her drooling? And the way she bites her hand? It wasn't that Michelle didn't love Jenny, but she hadn't forgotten other times when Jenny had embarrassed her. Like the noises she once made during the quiet part of the band concert that Michelle had played in. Or the puddle Jenny made last Easter when she peed in her wheelchair, right outside of church. . . .

Does your special sib drool? Make loud noises? Act or look unusual? If so, you may feel embarrassed when you are out in public together, or when friends come over to your house. You may be so embarrassed by your special sib that you don't invite your friends home (p. 6), or you avoid going out with your sib in public.

For most of us, like Michelle, being like everyone else is pretty important. A special sib can make that hard sometimes. Your sib may do things that seem strange and different. If this happens, try to remember that people's differences make the world interesting. Some people have different religions. Some have different skins colors. But they still have many things in common. Your sib may look different or walk differently from the way other children do, but he likes to watch the same television program as you do. He also likes to fly a kite and go for a boat ride on the lake. The ways in which people are the same are more important than how they differ.

If your sibling has embarrassing behavior problems, sometimes these problems can be helped by special programs (see "Behavior Problems," p. 47). You will probably want to ask your parents to help you work on your sib's embarrassing behavior problem. Let your parents know that there are certain things that your brother does that embarrass you, and ask them if the entire family could work on those things.

Other times, you may be embarrassed by things you *cannot* change, such as your sister's drooling, braces, crutches, or the way she looks. The stares and looks you get just walking with her in a shopping mall may make you feel uncomfortable. In fact, they may make you very unhappy, like Michelle. If this is the case, you may feel that for a while you need to detach yourself a little bit from her. That's okay. It doesn't mean you don't love her or that you aren't proud of her (see the section on "Pride," below). It doesn't mean that you won't want to spend time with her in public later on. But right now, you might need to put a little space—a little distance—between you and your sib. That's okay.

Pride

"You're proud of your sib's special qualities even if other people only see his handicaps."

"C'mon Tony! C'mon Tony!" shouted Charlie and Mike from the stands at the Special Olympics. On the field is their brother Tony, who is mentally retarded. Tony is short and round, but he was biting his lip and swinging his arms furiously as he raced toward the finish line.

"Yay! All right! Wa-hooie!" screamed Charlie and Mike as Tony crossed the finish line in second place. As soon as Tony stopped, he pushed up his glasses on his nose, looked at his brothers in the stands, smiled, and flashed a "V for victory" sign with his fingers.

On their way down to the field to congratulate him, Mike thought about what a neat kid Tony is. Sure, he could be a royal pain sometimes, but look what he did today! He couldn't remember ever being so proud of his little brother.

People who don't know someone who has a handicap often don't realize that people with handicaps have special qualities, just like anyone else. You often don't find out about these special qualities until you get to know a person. Because you and your family and your close friends know your sibling well, you know there are many things about her or him that make you proud. In fact, you feel proud of your sib for many of the same reasons that you feel proud of your other brothers and sisters—because your sib is good at some things, like swimming, or running, or playing wheelchair basketball, or saying things that make you laugh. And you also feel proud because you know how much extra effort it took for your sib to learn how to do some of these things.

Other people may only see what your special sib can't do. They see, for example, that your sister isn't as smart as her classmates, that she can't see, or can't walk without crutches. And that's all they see. But if they took the time to get to know her, they would understand why you and your family often feel like bragging.

For example, John's brother Dave has a learning disability. Dave has a very hard time spelling, reading, and writing. He has often had to stay inside and work on his homework when his friends were outside playing. Even though it has taken him longer than his classmates, Dave is learning to read, and he can now read some easy books all by himself. John and his family have watched him work on his reading while his friends were out playing. John has helped him. He knows how hard it has been for Dave to learn to read, because the letters of the alphabet get all mixed up for him. John feels very proud of Dave because he has tried so hard.

Or there is Susan's sister Jennifer, who is mentally retarded. Some of Susan's friends thought it was funny at first when Susan bragged about Jennifer, because Susan's friends knew that Jennifer was in the special class. They didn't think that there could be anything good about having a sister who is retarded. After all, Jennifer was lots slower than the other kids her age, and couldn't do many things, like multiply, or count money, or even play video games. She looked different, too. But now that some of Susan's friends have gotten to know Jennifer, they understand why Susan is so proud of her. She's proud of the way Jennifer takes care of her room now, waters the family's houseplants, and has learned to swim. Susan knows that these things are harder for Jennifer than for other girls her age. Knowing this makes her even prouder when Jennifer learns something new.

Mike couldn't remember ever being so proud of his little brother.

Gary has cerebral palsy. People often stare at him and feel sorry for him because he can't walk or talk. But his sister Sara knows that Gary can do some wonderful things, like writing messages on a special new computer attached to his wheelchair. Gary could not talk to people to let them know what he needed and what he was thinking before he got his special wheelchair. But now he can move his head to make the computer type out messages that others can read. Gary takes his special wheelchair to school and to the store. He can order a milkshake with it or do his homework on it. He can even play games on it. Sara knows that Gary has a great sense of humor and he often writes jokes on his computer. People who don't know Gary may feel sorry for him, but Sara has watched Gary learn to communicate, and she can think of many reasons to feel very proud of him.

Special sibs share these feelings of pride about their brothers and sisters who have special needs. They know that you have to look beyond what a person with a handicap can't do, and see what that person *can* do. Sibs also know that it takes time to appreciate the extra effort that goes into many of the ordinary things that a special sib learns how to do. People who don't take the time to get to know a person who is handicapped never find out how that person is changing and learning new things. And that's too bad, because they will never be able to share the feelings of pride that Dave's and Jennifer's and Gary's sibs enjoy.

Loss

*"Some things just won't be possible for your special sib.
Knowing that makes you sad."*

Tonight, sitting on her bed, Sally was feeling sad. Yesterday her brother Gene had left for college in another part of the state. That left Sally at home on the farm with her parents and her sister, Danielle, who is a year older than Sally, although you'd never know it. Danielle had some chromosome problem that Sally had never really understood.

Sally thought to herself: Even though Gene is older and we fight sometimes, at least we can talk. That's impossible with Danielle. Why can't I be like Jan? Jan and her sister do things together, share a room and tell each other about school, friends, and boys they like.

I wish I had a sister I could at least talk to, Sally thought as she stared out her bedroom window.

Did you ever want a game or a record for your birthday and get a sweater instead? At the time, you were probably disappointed. But after a while, you might have decided a sweater was okay. It *did* keep you warm, and it looked great with jeans. Still, you really wanted something else. In a way, you feel a sense of "loss," because you lost the thing you really wanted—the game.

Loss is a special sadness and disappointment people feel when something they wanted so much just isn't possible.

Siblings like Sally feel a sense of loss when they have a brother or sister who is handicapped. If your special sib is a baby, you may not be able to play with him the way you could if he weren't handicapped. If your handicapped sib is older than you, you may miss having an older brother or sister who can help you out and show you how to do things. Instead, *you* may have to teach your older handicapped sibling how to do things. You may also feel sad that your handicapped sibling cannot do all the things you can do, like ride a bike or go to a dance. Or like Sally you may miss having a brother or sister who can share secrets with you or give you advice. Sometimes you feel cheated because you miss out on things your friends enjoy with their brothers and sisters.

Your parents also felt a sense of loss when they first learned that your sib had a handicap. They had to give up some of the dreams they had for their child. Many things they wanted so much for all their children will not be possible for your special sib. They may have to accept that your sib will not go to college, or play basketball like your dad did, or get married and have a family.

It takes a long time for everyone in the family to get used to these losses. Sometimes it helps to tell someone—maybe your parents or a good friend or a trusted teacher—how you feel. Even if the other person can't change things, just sharing your feelings with someone you are close to can make you feel less sad.

Maturity

"Many adults who grew up with a handicapped sibling say they learned things that have made them wiser and stronger."

One evening Kerri was in her room getting ready to go to the movies with her friends. Her parents were also going out. It was their anniversary, and last week Kerri's mom had bought a new dress to wear to dinner.

The telephone rang and Kerri heard her mom answering it. Mrs. Randle, the baby-sitter, was calling to say that her daughter had just started to come down with the flu; she wouldn't be able to baby-sit with Lee that evening.

Kerri bit her lip. Lee, her brother, has epilepsy, like one of Mrs. Randle's children. Kerri's parents never worried when Mrs. Randle baby-sat for Lee. Ever since Kerri had started junior high, her parents had tried to get a baby-sitter for Lee on weekends so Kerri could go out with her friends.

Kerri heard her dad say he would have to call the restaurant and cancel their reservation for dinner. She came out of her room and said, "You and mom get your coats on or you'll be late. I'll stay and watch TV with Lee."

Kerri's mom gave her a big hug. The look of pride her dad gave her made her feel very grown up.

Today in Jerry's family life education class everyone was going to get a chance to feed a real baby. This year all the sophomores were taking the class, and they were learning such things as how to change diapers and how to hold babies the right way. Most of the girls did okay, but some of the boys got pretty nervous. Jerry's friend Sam looked scared when the teacher brought one of the babies over to their group. Jerry offered to be first and fed the baby some applesauce.

"How'd you get so good at that?" Sam asked. Jerry just shrugged. Jerry's sister Sue has cerebral palsy, and all the kids in his family had helped to feed and dress her and take her to the bathroom since she was a baby. Jerry didn't even think much about it. Everyone in the family had just learned to help Sue until she could do some of those things for herself.

Your life as a sibling of a child with special needs is different in some ways from the lives of your friends. You may have certain responsibilities, like Jerry does, for baby-sitting, feeding, or teaching your special sib. Your parents may trust you to do things that take extra patience, dependability, and time. You have probably already had to do some things that are much harder to do than things your friends have done—like answering a stranger's questions about your brother or sister, or giving up things you wanted to do, like Kerri, to take care of your sib. These experiences all add up to something called maturity, which means being grown up.

Many adults who grew up with a handicapped brother or sister say that their siblings helped them learn many things that made them stronger and wiser adults. They feel they are more understanding and patient as a result. These are qualities that make a person mature.

Your responsibilities and the way you've learned to think of others' needs have made you mature, like Kerri and Jerry. But too many responsibilities can prevent you from developing other qualities that are also important. Sometimes, parents of a child who is handicapped forget that their nonhandicapped children are not fully grown up, no matter how mature they may be.

If you feel that you spend too much time taking care of your special sibling and do not have time to do other things you would like to be doing, you should talk to your parents. It's important that no one in the family get overinvolved in caring for a handicapped family member. Every family member can do things to make it easier to care for a child with special needs. But all family members should have time for themselves, so they can do things they enjoy. And when everyone shares in the extra responsibilities, it's easier to give up something special once in a while, like Kerri did, to help out with your sib.

Worry

"If you have a handicapped brother or sister, you have different things to worry about than most of your friends."

Last month Allen's parents sat the whole family down and told them the bad news: their new little brother has Down syndrome. "He'll be just like us in almost every way," his mother told them, "except it will take him longer to learn. The doctor said that he'll probably be mentally retarded."
This year Allen is having a terrible time in math. He has almost flunked his last two tests. Today when he had a hard time again on his math test, Allen wondered: Maybe I'm retarded too?

Joan went with her family to an Association for Retarded Citizens family picnic last summer. At the picnic, Joan saw many handicapped adults. It made her think about her brother, who is retarded and has a heart problem: Will he live to grow up and go to school and get married? Or will his handicap get so bad that he dies?

At her cousin's wedding, Pam started thinking about her own future. Like her cousin, she wanted to get married and have children someday. Still, she wondered: If I have children, will they be deaf like my sister?

If you have a brother or sister who is handicapped, you have different worries from those of your friends. You probably have spent some time thinking about things that might happen to you or your sibling.

In the example above, Allen is worried that he might be mentally retarded like his brother. Since family members are alike in many ways, with the same color hair and eyes, and similar features, you may worry sometimes that you are like your handicapped sib. Strangers or other kids at school may say things about your special sib that hurt your feelings and make you wonder if

Joan thought about her little brother: Will he live to grow up,
or will his handicap get so bad he dies?

you are different too. Allen could stop worrying about this if he talked to his parents, teacher, or doctor about his brother's handicap. He would find out that mental retardation is not something you catch, like a cold, or something that all family members share. By talking to one of these people he could also find out what caused his brother's retardation, if the cause is known. This information could help him understand why his brother is retarded. Often, brothers and sisters of handicapped children just need to talk to someone to clear up something that is worrying them.

Like Joan, you may have spent some time worrying about what will happen to your handicapped brother or sister when you and your sib grow up. No one can ever tell for sure what a child will grow up to be like, especially a handicapped child. But we know enough about many handicaps to be able to know what happens to most children when they become adults. If you feel comfortable talking with your parents, ask them questions about the things that have been worrying you. You might also ask your teacher, family doctor, or school counselor.

If you are worried about who will take care of your sibling when he or she grows up, you need to ask your parents to sit down and talk to you about this. Often parents don't realize that the other children in the family are worried about the future (see p. 91). Your parents may have plans for your handicapped sib that they have not explained to you. Once you understand what your parents have planned for your brother or sister, you will feel better because you will know what your sib's life will be like when he or she grows up.

Like Pam, most siblings at one time or another worry about whether their own children will be handicapped. As we explain in Chapter 8, "The Future," this depends on what kind of handicap your sibling has. For example, if your sib has a certain kind of inherited condition, like cystic fibrosis or PKU, other children in your family may have children with PKU or cystic fibrosis even if they do not have the condition. If your sibling's handicap is hereditary, or if you are not sure what caused it, you should contact a genetics clinic. Your parents may already have this information and be able to share it with you. Genetics clinics are found in most medical schools and large hospitals. You can write to one of these two places to get the name of the genetics clinic nearest you:

>   March of Dimes
>   1275 Mamaroneck Avenue
>   White Plains, New York 10605
>
>   National Genetics Foundation, Inc.
>   250 West 57th Street
>   New York, New York 10019

Your doctor may also be able to help you understand what your chances are of having a child with a handicap.

Worries are like mushrooms. They grow best in dark places. Nothing gets rid of worries faster than to get them into the open. Parents and other grown-ups, like teachers and doctors, can often give you the facts that will explain away your worries. But sometimes it is hard to talk to your parents, and you need someone else to share your thoughts with. In some cities there are groups for siblings of children with special needs. They hold meetings, at which the siblings can get together to talk about the things that are on their minds. Your local Association for Retarded Citizens might be able to tell you if there is a group for siblings in your area. We talk about some ways to contact other siblings in the next section, on loneliness.

Loneliness

"It's easy to feel alone when there is no one to understand the special joys and challenges that you face daily."

When kids in his class start talking about their brothers or sisters, Jason gets very quiet. He doesn't say much about his special sister Erin. What would he say? Who would understand?

Suppose one girl bragged about how her brother won a prize at the Science Fair. What would Jason say? How proud he is that Erin, who is ten, can finally go to the bathroom by herself? Jason is proud of Erin all right, but they wouldn't understand.

If a classmate complained how her sister is always getting into her things, what could Jason say? That his father had to put a lock on his door to keep Erin out, because Erin doesn't know any better? Once she completely wrecked a model spaceship he had almost finished. No, his friends wouldn't understand.

Just once, Jason thought, I'd like to meet another kid who has a sister like Erin.

To feel lonely is to feel sad and different from your friends. Children, like Jason, who have special siblings can sometimes feel alone. They can feel that no one understands the special joys and challenges they face daily. You may not feel that you can talk about your special sib with your friends. Most of them don't know how it feels to have a sister who is retarded or who has cerebral palsy.

Parents with children who are handicapped can also feel lonely or isolated if they don't know other parents who face the same special concerns they do. Luckily, in many cities and towns there are groups where parents can meet other parents of handicapped children and talk about their worries and feelings. Being able to talk about things with someone who knows what you're going through can help you feel less lonely.

For some sibs, talking to their parents can help them feel less lonely. After all, parents know many of the special challenges children who are handicapped can cause for their sibs. But other families avoid talking about the special child's handicaps, because it is an uncomfortable topic for them to discuss.

When families avoid talking about the handicap, it can make sibs feel lonely because they can't discuss it with anyone who really knows what they are experiencing. It can also cause confusion, because sibs grow up without knowing much about their own brother's or sister's disability.

Everyone who has a person with special needs in the family should have someone to talk to who understands their feelings. If your parents can't or won't talk to you, try one of your other sibs, a favorite aunt, a grandparent, a teacher, or a friend. Another good way to feel less alone is to meet other kids your own age who have sibs with special needs.

It can be great to meet and talk with other sisters and brothers of children with special needs. They can understand your good feelings and bad feelings in a way that other friends can't. Just talking with them can make you feel less lonely. In some parts of the country, groups for siblings of children with special needs are starting to pop up. At these groups, sibs meet other sibs, talk, make new friends, and usually have a good time.

Unfortunately, some parts of the country don't have groups for sibs yet. If there isn't a sib group in your area, there are other ways to meet brothers and sisters of handicapped children. Ask your parents if your sister's or brother's school is having a picnic or party for the children's families that you and other sibs could attend. If not, tell them you would like to meet some other sibs. Ask them to help the school plan a picnic or a party. You can also ask your teacher or guidance counselor if they know any other sibs of special children in your school.

Books and other materials can help a sib feel less alone. In this book we talk about the feelings, joys, worries, and questions that sibs often have. There are many other books about siblings of children with specific handicaps, like blindness or cerebral palsy. At the end of this book is a list of books, about children with handicaps, that were written for young readers. It can help to curl up with one of these books and read about someone who has gone through some of the same things you are going through.

There are two other groups you should know about that can help you when you want to share your thoughts and worries. One is a group called SHARE for siblings of autistic children. If you write to this group, they will send you a newsletter, and they can help you find a pen pal who also has an autistic sibling. The second group puts out a newspaper called the SUN (which stands for Siblings Understanding Needs). This paper is written by children and teenagers with siblings who are handicapped or very sick. You might want to send for a copy or even write about your own experiences.

The addresses for these two groups are:

Siblings Helping Persons with Autism through Resources
and Energy (SHARE)
c/o NSAC
Suite 1017
1234 Massachusetts Avenue, N.W.
Washington D.C. 20005

Siblings Understanding Needs (SUN)
Department of Pediatrics C-19
University of Texas Medical Branch
Galveston, Texas 77550

There are also two groups for older siblings that are good information sources, the Sibling Information Network, and Siblings for Significant Change. The addresses for these two groups are in the Appendix.

In the following chapters we move from talking about feelings to facts. We present information to answer the most frequent questions siblings have about their brother's or sister's handicap, and the services and treatment available to help their special sib.

If you don't wish to read the whole book, check the table of contents for sections that are of special interest to you. Be sure to read the last chapter. It's all about you and your sib's future.

Chapter 2

Mental Retardation

We use the words "mental retardation" to talk about children who are slower than other children their own age. They are slower to learn things both in school and at home. Some children who are retarded will be able to learn to do many of the things you can do—like how to talk, ride a bike, and take a bus. It will just take them longer. Other children who are more retarded will not be able to learn these things.

If your brother is mentally retarded, you probably know how it affects him. He most likely took longer to learn to walk and talk than most children do. He may still not know how to walk and talk. Also, you know that it may take him a long time to learn other things—like how to stay out of your room, or count money at the store. If he is in school, he may be in a special class where the teacher can take more time to teach things such as how to read, count, tell time, and spell.

What Causes Mental Retardation?

Sometimes mental retardation is caused by something that happened before a child's birth. Handicaps that are caused by something before birth, such as Down syndrome (page 64), spina bifida (page 59), or Tay-Sachs disease (page

62), can cause mental retardation. If a woman who is pregnant has an accident, injury, serious disease, or is exposed to certain drugs, her child may be mentally retarded.

Premature birth, problems at birth, certain diseases, a poor environment, and accidents that cause brain damage (page 69) in a growing child sometimes cause mental retardation.

Aren't Some People More Retarded Than Others?

Not all those who are mentally retarded are the same. Because of this, people who are mildly retarded have different needs than people who are severely retarded. To make sure that children who are retarded get the kind of help they need, people who work with retarded persons talk about different levels of retardation.

Mild Retardation

Children who are mildly retarded learn more slowly than other children their age. They usually look like and can run and walk like anyone else. They may have more trouble than other people learning to talk, using their hands, following directions, and remembering things.

People who are mildly retarded may not seem different or slow, except in school, where they will have trouble learning in most subjects. But most are able to learn some reading, writing, math, and other academic skills. When they grow up, people who are mildly retarded have a good chance of holding a job and living independently. Many get married and have children.

Moderate Retardation

People who are moderately retarded learn things at a slower rate than people who are mildly retarded. As children, they are very slow to walk and talk. They can have trouble remembering things and are often clumsy. They have learning problems outside of school and need a lot more help learning to take care of themselves than other children do. Unlike mildly retarded children, who may not seem different from other children, a person who is moderately retarded will probably look or act different from other people. When they grow up, people who are moderately retarded may be trained to work in a sheltered workshop or at another simple job. They may live in a group home with other adults who are also retarded. Because of the complex and serious responsibilities involved in raising children, people who are moderately retarded usually do not become parents.

Severe and Profound Retardation

Children who are severely or profoundly retarded may never learn how to talk, and sometimes they do not learn how to walk. At school these children learn how to take care of themselves by learning how to eat, drink, and move around. These children usually have other handicaps in addition to mental retardation, such as epilepsy, cerebral palsy, problems seeing or hearing, or serious health problems. These children will need a lot of help for their many needs all of their lives. When they grow up, people who are severely or profoundly retarded may live in a group home or in the community. During the day they may attend a day activity center, where they can practice their skills and enjoy the company of other people. They may learn vocational skills that enable them to work in a sheltered workshop in their community.

Developmental Disability

Sometimes people who are mentally retarded are called "developmentally disabled." But even though all mentally retarded people are developmentally disabled, not all people with developmental disabilities are mentally retarded.

"Developmental disability" is an "umbrella" term that includes many handicaps that affect how a child grows and learns. Although most infants and children learn how to do things at about the same age, some children are much slower to learn things like crawling, walking, feeding, dressing themselves, and solving problems. These children have developmental disabilities. The federal government has an official definition of developmental disability that it uses to decide who can get special help like medical care and special education. According to the government, a developmental "delay" (disability) must be a severe and continual (chronic) condition which is a result of a mental or physical handicap, or both. The handicap must occur before the person's twenty-second birthday and be permanent. Common developmental disabilities are mental retardation, cerebral palsy, deafness, autism, and blindness.

How many retarded people are there?

For every 4,000 people in the world, approximately 100 are mentally retarded.

Mild **Moderate** **Severe**

For every 100 persons with mental retardation, approximately 85 have mild mental retardation, 12 have moderate mental retardation, and only 3 have severe or profound retardation. In the United States, there are approximately 6,500,000 (6½ million) people considered mentally retarded.

IQ (Intelligence Quotient)

Intelligence is another way of saying that a person is smart. The IQ score tells us how well a person did on an intelligence test. There are many different ways of measuring intelligence. Most psychologists (persons who study how the mind works) seem to agree that we are born with certain mental abilities. These abilities are influenced by what we experience in life.

There are many different tests that are used to measure intelligence. Most of these tests measure a child's abilities in areas such as arithmetic, vocabulary, memory, and social skills. When a psychologist tests a child's intelligence, she may ask the child to complete a sentence or a picture. She may ask the child to put together some objects in a certain way, or to solve an arithmetic problem. When a teacher gets a child's IQ score, the score and other information about the child can be used to plan the child's school program.

Some people say that intelligence tests are unfair because they favor some people over others. For example, language differences and different life-styles can make it harder for a black or Mexican-American child to do well on a test that was designed for white, middle-class children. Intelligence tests may favor people who are not handicapped, and they may not accurately reflect a handicapped child's actual abilities. Physical disabilities make it hard to measure a blind, deaf, or cerebral palsied person's intellectual potential— how well the person might do. There are some tests that give a fairer picture of a handicapped child's intelligence than other tests. Some tests can be used so that they do not underestimate the intelligence of a child who has a handicap.

An excellent source of information about mental retardation is your local Association for Retarded Citizens (ARC). This organization will be listed in your telephone book or you can write to the national office to obtain the address of your nearest ARC.

National Association for Retarded Citizens
2709 Avenue E East
P.O. Box 6109
Arlington, Texas 76011

Chapter 3

Handicaps That Affect How People See, Hear, Speak, Learn, and Behave

Handicaps affect the way we experience the world. As we explained in Chapter 2, mental retardation affects the way a child understands and gets along in his environment. The child with mental retardation is slower to learn and may not be able to learn many of the things that other children learn. Retardation limits the child's understanding and experience of the world.

Other handicaps affect the child's senses. We use our senses—especially sight, hearing, and speech—to take in information about our surroundings and to share our experiences. For example, we begin to use our eyes and ears when we are very young babies. The things that babies see and hear help them begin to understand how objects work and how people talk and act.

When one of the senses is affected by a handicap, we miss out on the information that we normally get from that sense. Children with a sensory handicap like blindness or deafness have to learn to use their other senses to collect information about the world.

Below we will describe the common sensory handicaps that affect vision, hearing, and speech. We will talk about learning disabilities, because these are also problems that make it hard for children to learn. We will also describe problems that affect the way a child acts, and suggest some ways of helping a sib who has a behavior problem, no matter what disability he or she has.

Vision Problems

What does the word "blind" really mean? My brother Michael is legally blind even though he can see some things. Some people don't think he can see at all.

You have probably heard someone describe how they see by mentioning numbers, such as 20/20 or 20/40. The numbers in the fraction refer to the Snellen chart. A person with 20/20 vision can read the figures in the Snellen chart at a distance of 20 feet. Someone who is legally blind has 20/200 vision or less with correction (glasses or contact lenses) in his or her better eye. This means that the person who is legally blind must be 20 feet away to read what

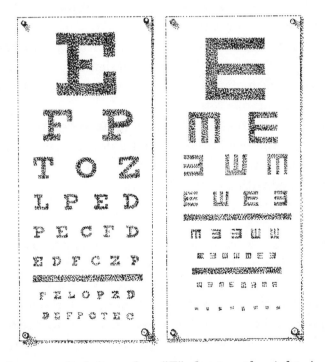

A Snellen eye chart, on the left, and an "E" chart on the right. A person reads down the Snellen chart as far as he can. A person who can read the bottom line from 20 feet has 20/20 vision. The "E" chart is used to test children and people who cannot read.

someone with normal vision (20/20) can read at 200 feet. A person who is legally blind is not necessarily totally blind. Most people who are legally blind can see enough to perform some tasks.

Some infants are born blind or with partial loss of vision. When babies are born with vision problems, they have what is called a *congenital* vision problem. Sometimes it may be caused by an infection that the mother had during her pregnancy, such as German measles. Some forms of vision loss are inherited, and can be passed from the parents to the child. If a child inherits a vision loss, the parents may also have a vision loss, or they may be carriers for the condition that causes the loss. Some infants who are born with a certain syndrome (see p. 64) may have a visual handicap.

Some children lose their sight after birth. The most common cause of blindness in the United States is *cataracts*. These are a clouding of the lens of the eye. Cataracts may be found in children who are born with German measles or with Down syndrome (see p. 64). An injury to the eye can also result in cataracts. These can be treated surgically by removing the lens of the eye and replacing it with a substitute lens.

Many premature infants who receive too much oxygen after they were born develop *retrolental fibroplasia* (RLF) (rĕt-trō-leń-tal fĭ-brow-plaý-sha), which sometimes causes permanent blindness. Too much oxygen will damage the blood vessels in an infant's retina.

Another cause of blindness is *glaucoma* (glaw-coé-ma). When a person has glaucoma, fluid in the eye builds up and damages the inside of the eye. A person may be born with glaucoma or may develop it during childhood. Glaucoma is treated with eye drops or surgery.

I have to wear glasses, even though my vision is not too bad. What causes vision problems like mine?

Mild vision problems often result from changes in the normal shape of the eyeball that prevent light rays from focusing properly on the retina. When the eyeball is too long, the person has *myopia* (my-opé-ee-ya), or nearsightedness, and can't see clearly things that are far away. When the eyeball is too short, the person has *hyperopia* (hy-pur-opé-ee-ya), or farsightedness. These problems can be corrected with glasses or contact lenses.

My brother's eyes look in different directions. What makes this happen?

Other vision problems are caused when the muscles that move the eye do not work together. *Strabismus* (stra-biź-muss) is the inability to focus both eyes on the same object. The eyes send two separate pictures to the brain rather than one. The brain responds by gradually ignoring all the images from the weaker eye. This results in *amblyopia* (ăm-blee-opé-ee-ya), a loss of vision in the eye that grows weak from not being used. Amblyopia can be treated when the child is young by putting a patch over the strong eye. This forces the weak eye to get stronger. Special exercises also help to strengthen the weak eye.

Blindness is very uncommon in children. Only one out of every 2,500 children is blind. About half of the children who are blind are born with their handicap, and about 40 percent lose their sight before they are one year old. One-fourth of blind children have no sight at all; the rest can detect light or see well enough to read very large letters. It is fairly easy to identify an infant who is totally blind. Normally babies use their sense of sight to follow objects, reach for toys, and smile at their families. Infants who are totally blind will not do these things. It is more difficult to tell when an infant has a less serious vision problem. People who test how well babies see do this by watching how they move their eyes, how they reach for toys, or how well they recognize pictures.

The loss of sight in the infant and young child will slow the child's development. The child probably won't learn to sit up, crawl, or walk at the same age as the child with normal vision. For example, children who are blind do not reach out for objects until about four months later than children who can see. The blind child may not talk until much later than the sighted child. Children who are blind may have unusual behavior: they may rock back and forth, or bang their heads. Such behavior is called self-stimulatory behavior. The child who is blind will do these things if he or she is not trained to use other senses and to learn new skills. Children who are blind and children with vision problems need extra help to learn many of the things that children with sight learn just by looking at the world around them. For example, because blind infants cannot see that their actions affect things around them, they need to be helped to move and to play with different toys and objects. Some things that you take for granted are very hard for blind children to understand. They need extra help to learn that objects exist even when they are not playing with them. They need to touch things and feel how objects fit together. It is also important that children who are blind hear the words for the things around them so that they can learn to talk.

If you want more information on blindness and visual handicaps, you may want to write to:

American Foundation for the Blind, Inc.
15 West 16th Street
New York, New York 10011

Hearing Problems

There are several terms that are used to describe persons with hearing losses. A person who is *deaf* has a hearing loss so great that he or she cannot hear what is being said, even with a hearing aid. A person who is *hard of hearing* can usually hear what is being said with the use of a hearing aid. Persons with less severe hearing losses have varying degrees of difficulty hearing what others say.

Some infants are born deaf, while other people lose their hearing later in life. There are three main causes of deafness in infants: genetic reasons, disease, or trauma (an injury). About 40 to 60 percent of all deafness is genetic. This means it is passed from the parents to the child. If a child inherits a gene (see "Birth Defects," p. 52) from the parents that causes deafness, we say that the child's deafness is genetic in origin. Certain diseases and injuries also cause deafness. German measles is the most common virus that can cause deafness. Mothers who have German measles in the first three months of their pregnancy are most likely to have a child who is deaf or who has a serious hearing loss. Meningitis (see p. 71) is an infection that causes about 10 percent of all deafness. Children who have frequent infections in their middle ear may suffer permanent hearing losses. Children with Down syndrome often get these infections. Some drugs taken by a pregnant mother or young child may cause deafness. A head injury, high fever, exposure to very loud noises, or a difficult birth are other causes of deafness. Of all the cases of deafness, the causes are not known for about half.

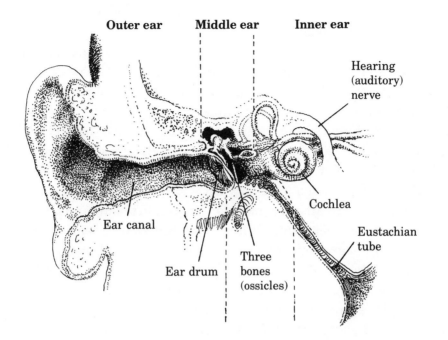

Hearing losses can be caused by problems in the outer, middle, or inner ear.

How much we can help a person to hear depends on the part of the ear that is affected by the causes listed above. Some hearing losses are the result of problems in the outer or the middle part of the ear. When the outer or middle ear has problems, sound doesn't reach the inner ear. This can often be helped with a hearing aid. Sometimes the hearing problem is in the inner ear or in the nerve that sends sounds to the brain. This kind of loss usually cannot be corrected. A mixed loss is a combination of problems in the outer or middle ear and the inner ear. A person with a mixed loss may be helped with a hearing aid.

Why don't all people with hearing problems just wear hearing aids?

A hearing aid amplifies sounds (makes them louder). When sounds can't reach the inner ear, a hearing aid can make the sounds louder and easier to receive. But the inner ear must be able to translate these sounds into messages the brain can read. This is why a hearing aid would not help a person with an inner ear problem.

There are some other words that may be used when someone describes your sib's hearing problem. A person with a *mild* hearing loss is able to hear all the sounds of normal speech. A person with a *moderate* loss can hear some sounds, and a person with a *severe* loss cannot hear normal speech.

A child who has a *congenital* hearing loss is born deaf or hard of hearing. A congenital loss has the most serious effect on the child's language skills, because in the first few years of life the child learns to talk by listening to others. Deaf children often have very little speech and less developed social skills. Language skills are very important in a child's home and school life. So it is very important that young children who cannot hear learn to communicate through sign language or a combination of signs and speech. In order to help children who are deaf learn to communicate, parents, brothers, and sisters need to learn sign language too. Early medical treatment and education also help the child use whatever hearing remains.

One very good source for information on deafness is:

Gallaudet College
Florida Avenue and 7th Street N.E.
Washington, D.C. 20002

Speech and Language Problems

Aren't speech and language problems the same thing?

Although people often use the words "language" and "speech" interchangeably, they really mean two different things. The word "language" includes many types of communication, like speaking, reading, writing, facial expressions, body language, and other ways of sharing thoughts and feelings. Speech is making words with your mouth, lips, teeth, tongue, vocal cords, and lungs. Speech is only one part of language. A child may have speech problems or language problems, or he may have both.

A *speech problem* makes it difficult for a child to talk and be understood. One common speech problem is stuttering. People who stutter may make sounds longer ("Thhhat's my dog"); or they may repeat sounds ("Wh-wh-where is my mom?"), syllables ("I'm go-going to-to-tomorrow"), or whole words ("Can can can Mike come to to play?"). People who stutter don't stutter on every word, and many can use their voice in ways so they sometimes don't stutter. For instance, Mel Tillis, the country-western singer, has a stuttering problem that doesn't affect his singing. Stuttering may be mild or severe. Although the cause of stuttering is not known, speech therapy for stuttering can be very helpful.

A child with *articulation* (are-tick-yoo-lay'-shun) *problems* is hard to understand, and sounds different from other children who are the same age and speak the same language. A child whose mouth or throat has an unusual shape may have articulation problems. These problems make it hard for the child to form words. For instance, a person with a cleft lip and palate may be hard to understand because of the shape of his palate and lip. Difficulty controlling the muscles that produce speech can also cause articulation problems; people with cerebral palsy (p. 73) often have difficulty saying words clearly. Children with *developmental articulation problems* have nervous systems that are immature ("too young") for their age. Because their nervous systems are not as well developed as those of other children their age, it is difficult for them to speak accurately so others understand them.

A child with a *language problem* may have trouble understanding what other people say, talking to other people, or both. Children who have trouble understanding what they hear have a *receptive problem*. They may not understand anything that is said to them, or they may understand single words only. Children with a receptive problem may have trouble following directions.

Because people must be able to hear before they can talk, children with receptive problems (problems understanding what they hear) often have *expressive problems* (problems talking). For example, a girl with an expressive problem may know how to say only a few words. She may not know the words for certain items, or may use the wrong word. She may not use grammar rules that other children her age use. For example, she may say "Me want" instead of "I want that toy."

Many children who have language and speech problems have no other handicaps. But children with certain handicaps are more likely to have problems with their speech or language. As we have mentioned, people with cerebral palsy, cleft palate and lip, and developmental disabilities may have speech problems because they cannot form the words so that others can easily understand them. Children with Down syndrome may have articulation problems because they have poor muscle control. Children with hearing losses, mental retardation, emotional disturbance, or hyperactivity may have receptive language problems because they can't process what they hear.

Learning Disabilities

My little sister Rachel has a learning disability and needs special help in school. Some kids call her retarded, because she goes to a special class. I know she's not retarded, because she's really smart in a lot of ways. What exactly is a learning disability?

Learning disabilities (LD) include many different problems that children may have in learning. These learning differences make it hard for some children to listen, talk, think, read, or do math. A learning disability is different from mental retardation (see p. 29). A child who is mentally retarded is slower than normal in all mental activities. A child with a learning disability may have a high, medium, or low IQ. The child may do well in some areas, like reading, and poorly in other areas, like math. Most of us are weak in some areas, like being able to dribble a basketball, or ice skate, or sing on key. These weaknesses are not considered learning disabilities, because they do not usually affect how well we do in school. A learning disability makes it hard for a child to do well in school. In addition, it often affects the way the child behaves in and out of school.

Children with learning disabilities often differ from other children in two ways: they often have learning and behavior problems. We will describe these problems:

Learning problems: It may take longer than normal for the child with a learning disability to learn how to talk, how to read, or how to solve math problems. The child may have trouble paying attention to letters, remembering words, or putting sentences together. The child may not be able to keep up

*A person with a learning disability may do well in some areas,
but have a hard time in others.*

with the rest of his or her classmates in arithmetic, or be able to remember the important ideas in a story.

Behavior problems: Some children with learning disabilities are very active. Because they have a hard time paying attention, they get restless, and they may not do what they have been told to do. Other children with learning disabilities are slow and disorganized. They may start out to do one thing, forget what they were doing, and begin to do something else.

When your sibling has a learning disability, it can affect other people in your family. If your brother or sister sleeps poorly, your parents may get tired and irritable from having to get up at night. Everyone in your family is likely to get irritated and impatient if your sib is very slow and never seems to be dressed in time to go to school, or is often late for dinner. Your sib may upset family and friends with temper tantrums.

Children with learning disabilities may have trouble making friends and getting along with other children. If they are clumsy, other children may not want to play games with them. They may sometimes forget the rules. Or they may embarrass their family and friends by saying the wrong things, or making a scene in public. Family members can all do something to help the child with learning disabilities get along better. It is important that the child learn to do things independently. Family members can organize life to help the child remember what to do. If your brother is always late for school, someone can check to be sure his clothes and schoolbag are laid out the night before. If he cannot remember things, you must give him very simple directions. For example, if you tell him to go to the store to buy milk and bread, he may go to the store but come back with only the bread, because he forgot what he was supposed to bring home. He may need to make a list to help him remember. Although your family cannot do everything for your brother, they can find ways to help him do things for himself.

No one knows exactly what causes these differences in learning. Children with learning disabilities often come from families with a history of learning problems. Learning disabilities are more common in boys than in girls.

Just as learning disabilities vary from child to child, each child's future will be different. Some children with learning disabilities are able to work very hard to complete academic programs in high school so that they can go on to college. Other children go to schools that teach trades or job skills, or they enter fields where they do not need to use the reading or math skills that are so hard for them to learn.

Autism (ŏtt´-iz-ŭm)

My brother Sam is four years old but he still doesn't talk. Sometimes he'll repeat what you say to him, but most of the time he acts as though he doesn't even hear you. My parents say he is autistic.

Autism is a lifelong *developmental disability* (see p. 31) that prevents a person from correctly understanding what he or she sees, hears, or senses. Autism occurs in about five out of every 10,000 births. It is usually identified in the child's first three years of life. An autistic person usually has severe problems learning, communicating, and behaving.

Children with autism may have strange ways of relating to people and objects. They may have very unusual responses to sound, sight, touch, or pain. Sometimes people with autism are slow in learning to talk, do not speak at all, or only repeat what they have heard. People with severe forms of autism may repeat certain actions over and over.

It is thought that autism results from brain damage. Although the causes of this damage are not clearly understood, it has been found that many children with autism were born too early, had other problems at birth, or had infections that hurt the brain. Since these problems can also cause mental retardation (p. 29) or cerebral palsy (p. 73), a person with autism may also have these conditions. It is *not* thought that autism is caused by a child's relationship with his or her parents, or by other psychological or environmental problems.

Most, but not all, autistic people are also mentally retarded. Special education programs that teach children with autism to control their behavior have been shown to be helpful for the child and family.

Hyperactivity

My brother Bobby is hyperactive. We call him the Human Tornado, because he's always moving and messing up things. He gets in trouble a lot and is hard to live with. What can we do to help him slow down?

A child who is hyperactive (superactive) may always seem to be moving and "on the go." He may run up and down the aisles when he goes shopping with his mother. He may not be able to sit in one place or do one thing for more than a few minutes. Children who are hyperactive have trouble controlling their actions. They cannot pay attention for very long. (They are sometimes called attention deficient, which means they do not have enough attention, and they are easily distracted from what they are doing.) They may fidget and get restless when they have to sit in one place. They may jump up and down a lot, going from one thing to another. Parents and siblings of a child who is hyperactive often have to watch the child constantly to be sure he doesn't hurt himself.

Hyperactivity often becomes a serious problem when the child goes to school. Because the child cannot pay attention, he has great difficulty doing school work, like reading or listening to a lesson. He will often forget what the teacher tells him, or will only hear the first part of what someone says to him. He may have other learning problems that make it hard to copy letters or learn to write. He may do so poorly in school that he stops trying and gives up. Or he may get angry because he can't learn, and because his teachers and parents are unhappy with his work. He may have tantrums. He may get bad marks in conduct because he acts out in class.

Hyperactivity is more common in boys than in girls. Children who are hyperactive may have a hard time getting along with other children. Because children who are hyperactive are often clumsy, their classmates may not ask them to play with them. Other children may call them retarded even though children who are hyperactive usually have normal IQs (see p. 33) and are just as smart as other children their own age.

There are many causes of hyperactivity, and the exact causes of a child's problems may not be known. It may be caused by brain damage (see p. 69). There are many ways to help hyperactive children. In the section on behavior problems (see p. 47) we describe several ways to help children learn to control their own behavior. Children who are hyperactive seem to do better when rules are short and clear. Special education and counseling may also help the child who is hyperactive. Hyperactivity is sometimes treated with medicine that calms the child down and helps him or her pay attention. Some children outgrow their hyperactivity as they get older. A child may have fewer problems when he leaves school and no longer needs to sit in one place and pay attention for long periods of time.

Emotional Disturbance

I feel sorry for my sister Janet. She keeps to herself almost all the time and looks sad. She doesn't have any friends. My parents say she is emotionally disturbed.

A child who is emotionally disturbed acts differently from the way other children do. For example, an emotionally disturbed girl may not act the way we usually think someone should act in a particular place or at a particular time. She may not make friends and may frequently be unhappy or sad and depressed. She may often be angry and fight a lot; may have frequent tantrums; may be afraid for no reason; may hit other children; may act "silly"; may not be able to control how she acts; or may be very withdrawn. She may not talk to anyone or try to play with other children.

There are many different reasons why a child may be emotionally disturbed. Often the exact cause for the child's behavior is not known. The child's actions often create stress for all those around him or her. The child may not be able to learn and may have trouble making friends.

There are several different ways of changing the way an emotionally disturbed child behaves. Some of these ways are described in the next section on behavior problems. For example, a teacher or a parent might encourage the child to act differently by: changing the setting in which the child has problems behaving correctly; telling the child how you expect him to act; making sure the child understands the rules that he should follow at a certain time; giving the child many opportunities to do things that he likes to do and does well; and always rewarding and praising the child when he or she does the right thing. Families can use some of these ideas to help the emotionally disturbed child act differently in the home.

Behavior Problems

My brother is always bugging me when I'm trying to watch TV or mess around with my friends. How can I make him stop?

How many times have you heard your parents or teacher say "Behave yourself!" or "Quit misbehaving!" Learning how to behave, or act correctly, is part of growing up. Although it's sometimes hard to learn how to behave, most of us learn eventually.

Some children have an extremely hard time learning how to behave. They may have special behavior problems that make life very difficult for them and the people around them. Below we suggest some ways of helping with a sib's behavior problem, regardless of his or her disability.

Behavior modification is one way of changing the way a person acts. Behavior is something a person does that we can see—an action performed. For example, "being nice" or "being mean" is not an action, but "sharing a toy" or "pulling hair" is. "To modify" means to change. Behavior modification is a way of rewarding the actions we like and discouraging those we don't like.

Sometimes behavior modification is used at home and at school with children who have special needs. The term "behavior modification" usually refers to a carefully written plan for rewarding or changing behavior, but, in fact, our behavior is "modified" all the time. Here are two examples of how rewards can change behavior: If you were to juggle at a school assembly and received a standing ovation, you'd be likely to want to juggle in public again. If your mom makes a chocolate cheesecake for dessert, and after dinner you hug her and tell her it was the best cheesecake you've ever eaten, she would probably be more likely to behave (make a chocolate cheesecake) that way again. The two actions, juggling and baking a cheesecake, were "positively reinforced." You can use positive reinforcement to help you get your brother or sister to behave in better ways.

Positive Reinforcement

When you reward behavior that you want to happen *more* often, you are using positive reinforcement. We get positively reinforced in many ways—a hug from our parents for cleaning our room, praise from a friend for a high score on a video game, or money from the next-door neighbor for mowing her grass. We all have different ways we like to be reinforced or rewarded. Your handicapped brother may enjoy receiving applause or a hug when he does something you want him to do, such as putting on his own socks or going to the bathroom by himself.

Positive reinforcement not only must make a person happy, it also must *increase* the chances that the person will act that way again. For example, you might promise your sister five minutes of "special time" with you in your room if she helps you do the dishes. You would use this special time as a positive reinforcer. But if your sister doesn't help with the dishes in the future, "special time" would not be a good reinforcer, even if she *did* enjoy it. You would have to try another reinforcer, like reading her a story, or letting her play with one of your toys. A good reinforcer makes the person want to do a certain action more in the future.

You can use different things, like hugs or kind words, as reinforcers to increase good behavior. But what do you do about behavior you *don't* want? Ignoring it may help a lot.

Ignoring

One day Janet went up to her best friend Cheryl at school and tried to talk to her. Instead of responding, Cheryl did not look at Janet or talk to her. If you were Janet, what would you do? You might try again a few times, but after a while you'd probably quit trying to talk to Cheryl.

When someone ignores you, you probably stop doing what you are doing in regard to that person, or you try doing something else. This is why ignoring can be a powerful way to stop behavior we don't like. In the last example, Janet's behavior— talking—was stopped because Cheryl ignored her.

Here is an example of how you can stop your sibling from doing something you don't like by ignoring your sib's behavior. When Stephen does not get his way, he screams and cries. Tired of hearing him scream, his sister gives him what he wants. In the future Stephen continues to scream and cry for what he wants. Although she may not know it, Stephen's sister is rewarding his screaming and crying. He would be more likely to stop screaming if she ignored him. Now when Stephen screams, everyone ignores him. After a while Stephen will scream less and less, because he does not get rewarded with attention when he screams.

You should know that when you first begin to ignore behavior you don't like, such as Stephen's screaming, the unwanted behavior will probably *increase* for a while before it decreases. Stephen will probably scream louder and longer the first few times he is ignored, as if to say "Can't you hear me? Let me turn up the volume." He will do this because he is used to getting attention when he screams. So now he'll try harder. It's important to continue ignoring him when he does this. If you give in to him, even one time, he'll learn that all he has to do is scream longer and louder to get what he wants.

Ignoring can be effective, but it can also be difficult. You have to remember that what you *don't* do is as important as what you do. When you ignore, you don't talk, touch, answer questions, or look at the person you are ignoring. You do this for as long as they continue to do what you want them to stop doing. If you are ignoring your sister and she tries to climb into your lap or take you by the hand, you must remove her and do something else. It is also important to reward her for doing what you want her to do. After she quits screaming and crying, you should remember to say something nice, like "It's much easier to talk to you when you're not crying," and then pay attention to her.

You can use behavior modification with your handicapped sib, or with your parents, friends, or teachers. Everyone likes positive reinforcement, even though people are reinforced by different things. What does your sib like? Praise? Hugs? Visits to your room or other special privileges? Use these when you want to reward your sib for good behavior. Make it a point to look for good behavior and reward it.

It used to be that when Stephen cried, his parents and sister would give him whatever he wanted. Now they ignore his screaming. As a result, he screams less and less, because his screaming is not rewarded with attention.

Ignoring is a good technique to use for undesirable attention-getting behavior such as throwing a tantrum, teasing, and pestering. Be sure to do a good job ignoring, and reward your sib when she acts appropriately.

If your sibling's behavior is causing you problems that you can't ignore, tell your parents. Your sib's teacher can probably help you set up a more intense behavior modification program that you and your family can try. A book that can help parents set up a behavior modification program for a child with special needs is *Behavior Problems* by Bruce L. Baker, Alan J. Brightman, et al., Research Press, 2612 North Mattis Ave., Champaign, Illinois 61820

Chapter 4

Handicaps
Children Are Born With

Birth Defects

Many children are born with their handicaps. These handicaps result from a birth defect. A birth defect, sometimes called a congenital (cŏn-jĕń-nă-tal) defect, is one that is present at the infant's birth. It may be caused by problems a child inherits from his parents, by something in the environment (such as infection, or exposure to certain drugs or chemicals during pregnancy), or by a combination of the two. Many times we don't know what caused a congenital or birth defect.

Is there any way to find out before the baby is born if it will have a birth defect?

Amniocentesis (ăḿ-nee-ō-sĕn-teé-sis) is a medical procedure that helps the doctor tell if the unborn fetus (the unborn infant is called a fetus from the time it is eight weeks old until it is born; before that it is an embryo) has certain birth defects. Amniocentesis also tells the doctor the sex of the unborn child. The procedure gets its name from the amniotic fluid that surrounds the developing fetus. This fluid is studied to identify possible problems, like spina bifida (see p. 59), Down syndrome (see p. 64), or Tay-Sachs disease (see p. 62).

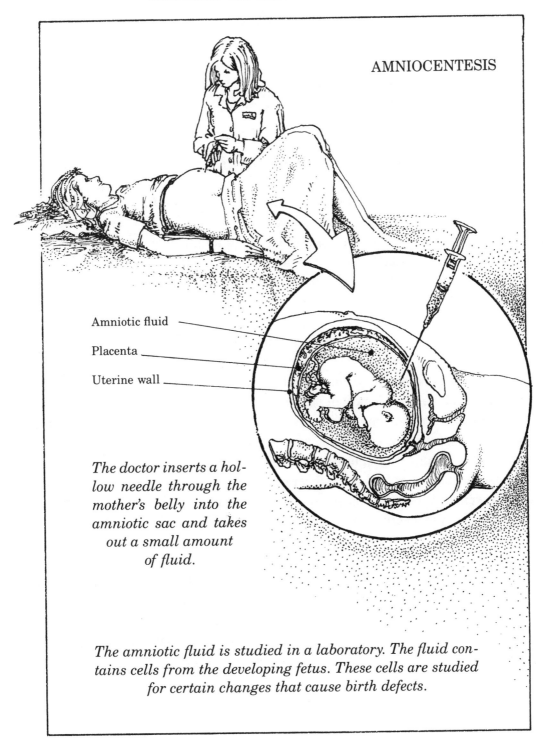

AMNIOCENTESIS

Amniotic fluid

Placenta

Uterine wall

The doctor inserts a hollow needle through the mother's belly into the amniotic sac and takes out a small amount of fluid.

The amniotic fluid is studied in a laboratory. The fluid contains cells from the developing fetus. These cells are studied for certain changes that cause birth defects.

Amniocentesis is usually done when the woman is 16 to 18 weeks pregnant. The doctor inserts a hollow needle through the mother's belly into the amniotic fluid and takes out a small amount of fluid. This fluid is studied in a laboratory. The fluid contains cells from the developing fetus. These cells are studied for irregularities that cause birth defects.

Won't the needle hurt the baby or the mother?

The needle doesn't hurt the mother. Before the mother has amniocentesis, the doctor often uses ultrasound to picture where the baby is. Ultrasound uses sound waves to picture the baby, like a bat or a submarine uses sound waves to locate things in the dark. When the doctor can see where the baby is, he can put the needle in a place where it will not hurt the baby.

Do all pregnant women have to have amniocentesis?

A doctor may recommend amniocentesis if a pregnant woman is over thirty-five years old, because a mother's chance of having a baby with a birth defect (such as Down syndrome) increases as she gets older. A doctor may also recommend amniocentesis if the woman has had previous miscarriages (has lost her baby early in pregnancy), if she has had a relative with an inherited disease, or if she has had a handicapped child. When amniocentesis reveals that a woman is going to have a child with a severe birth defect or a serious disease, she may begin to make special plans for her child's future needs, or she may decide not to have the child.

Amniocentesis may be performed if there is a family history of a certain handicap. Many of these problems, such as Tay-Sachs disease, can be diagnosed before birth. Some handicaps—only a very few—can be treated before the child's birth. Not all handicaps can be diagnosed with amniocentesis. This is why sometimes a woman may have a handicapped baby even though she had a normal amniocentesis when she was pregnant.

What causes birth defects?

One of the most common questions siblings ask is why their baby brother or sister was born with a handicap. Many times no one knows the answer. Sometimes doctors can trace the cause to a change in the baby's chromosomes, to something the mother was exposed to when she was pregnant, or to something the father was exposed to before the baby was conceived.

Birth Defects Caused by Chromosome Changes

Normal cells in your body have 46 chromosomes, except for the male's sperm cells and female's egg cells. These cells have only 23 chromosomes. When the egg is fertilized, cells divide and multiply as the baby is growing inside the pregnant mother. Some handicaps, like Down syndrome (see p. 64), occur when the cells divide the wrong way. In most cases, the problem occurs before the egg and the sperm cell join, and either the egg or the sperm cell did not divide normally. When this happens, an egg or a sperm cell may have 24 instead of 23 chromosomes. If an egg with 24 chromosomes is fertilized by a sperm with 23 chromosomes, the child will have 47 chromosomes and will have Down syndrome. In other cases, the problem can occur shortly after the egg and sperm join and then divide the wrong way. This will leave some cells with 47 chromosomes, while most will have the normal 46.

Birth Defects Caused by Things in the Environment

Other birth defects result from the mother's or father's exposure to something in the environment, or from a combination of things in the environment and things that are inherited from the parents. As we said, many times the exact cause of a birth defect is not known. Certain things may interfere with the normal cell divisions during the mother's pregnancy. Radiation may cause birth defects. X rays are radiation. That is why pregnant women must be very careful when they receive x rays.

Normal body cells
contain 46 chromosomes.

1	2	3	4	5
6	7	8	9	10	11	12
13	14	15	16	17	18
19	20	21	22	23

A nonhandicapped child's
chromosomes, organized and
numbered for study.

1	2	3	4	5
6	7	8	9	10	11	12
13	14	15	16	17	18
19	20	21	22	23

DOWN SYNDROME

The chromosomes of a child
with Down syndrome. There is an
extra chromosome on the 21st pair.

Certain infections and viruses may also produce birth defects. For example, pregnant women who are exposed to German measles have a high risk of having a child with several birth defects.

Some drugs and chemicals cause birth defects. We now know that women who smoke cigarettes or who drink alcohol are more likely to have infants who are born with mental and physical defects.

The timing of the mother's exposure to something harmful in her environment will determine how the infant is affected. If she is exposed at the beginning of her pregnancy, her exposure is likely to result in a defect that affects the baby's brain, or the arms and legs, which develop at that time. Exposure during the middle of the mother's pregnancy may affect the child's eyes, and exposure at the end may damage the child's brain or muscles.

Common Birth Defects

My brother has a birth defect, and so does my friend's sister, but they are so different. How many kinds of birth defects are there?

There are many kinds of birth defects. Some are very rare. Below we will discuss some of the more common ones.

Microcephaly (my-crow-séf-a-lee)

A child with microcephaly ("small brain") has a smaller than normal head and is usually mentally retarded. The exact cause of microcephaly is often not known. Possible causes include certain disorders a child gets from its parents, or a syndrome such as Down syndrome. Microcephaly can also be caused by the mother's exposure to radiation (the energy given off by x rays), certain drugs, infections, or anoxia (see p. 68), which is a lack of enough oxygen for the infant at the time of birth.

Hydrocephalus (hy-drō-séf-a-lus)

The origins of this word are hydro (water) plus cephalus (head). This condition results when fluid builds up in the brain. Normally, fluid circulates between the brain and spinal column. A birth defect, an early injury, or an illness may stop the fluid from circulating and cause it to collect in the brain. The fluid then presses on the brain cells and nerves. Children with hydrocephalus may be mentally retarded, paralyzed (unable to move part of their body), or have seizures (see p. 77) as a result of the pressure. Hydrocephalus often occurs in children with spina bifida (see below). It may also result from a head injury, or an infection like meningitis (see p. 71).

Hydrocephalus is treated by inserting a small tube, called a shunt, in the child's head. This tube drains the excess fluid from the brain. It prevents fluid and pressure from building up and damaging the brain. Siblings often ask where the water goes when the tube is put in. The tube drains the extra water into other parts of the body, where it will not collect as it does in the brain.

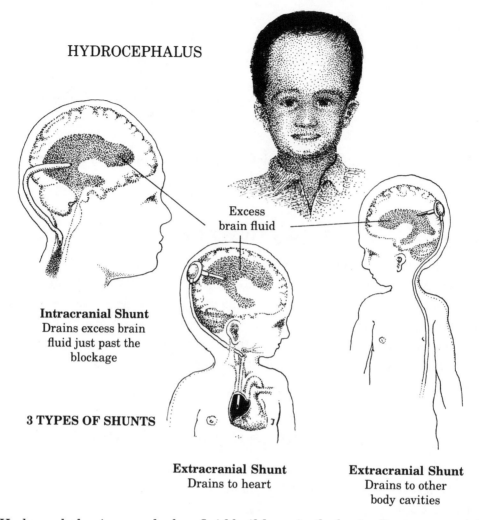

HYDROCEPHALUS

Excess
brain fluid

Intracranial Shunt
Drains excess brain
fluid just past the
blockage

3 TYPES OF SHUNTS

Extracranial Shunt
Drains to heart

Extracranial Shunt
Drains to other
body cavities

Hydrocephalus is caused when fluid builds up in the brain. Doctors treat it by inserting a shunt, or tube, which drains the fluid into other parts of the body. There are several different types of shunts that may be used.

If hydrocephalus is not treated, the fluid will increase the pressure within the infant's head, causing it to expand by pushing open the bones of the infant's soft skull. As the child develops, the bones around the brain harden. When hydrocephalus occurs in an older child, there is no room for the brain to expand inside its hard, bony case. The increased pressure can cause serious problems if the condition is not treated.

Spina Bifida (spý-na bí-fi-dă)

This is a birth defect that is caused when the spinal cord does not develop properly. Spina bifida is Latin for split spine. Normally, when the mother is three to four weeks pregnant, the embryo's nervous system begins to develop. A layer of cells thickens and forms a groove. This groove closes to form the neural tube, which will become the child's brain and spinal cord. Later, the backbones grow around the neural tube to protect the delicate nerves inside.

Sometimes, for reasons we do not understand, the backbones do not close to

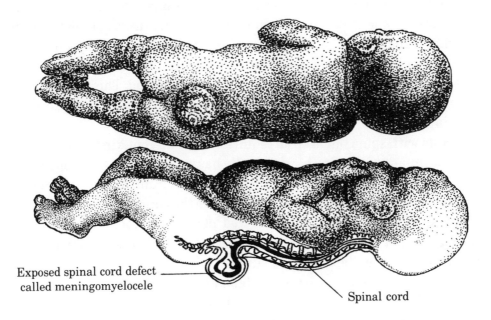

Exposed spinal cord defect called meningomyelocele

Spinal cord

Spina bifida occurs when the spinal cord does not develop properly, and part of the spinal cord is exposed.

Normally, this is how the spinal cord develops and becomes encased in the neural tube, which becomes the child's backbone. The neural tube and later the backbone protect the delicate nerves inside

Neural plate   Neural fold   Neural groove   Neural tube closed protect the spinal cord. Part of the spinal cord or its covering sticks out from the opening in the backbone. The nerves that go to this open part of the spinal cord don't work the way they should. This may mean that the nerves that send messages to the legs don't work, and the child can't walk.

Siblings often ask why spina bifida is different in different people. This is because the birth defects depend on where the opening is on the child's spinal cord. The higher up on the spinal cord the defect is located, the more severe the handicap. When the spinal cord is open, the nerves that send signals to other parts of the body are damaged. A defect on the upper part of the spinal cord will affect more nerves than a defect that is lower. Some children with spina bifida may have very weak arm and leg muscles, or may be completely paralyzed. The child's back and feet may change shape when certain muscles are not used. Some children with spina bifida do not have complete control when they urinate. Another serious problem that can result from spina bifida is hydrocephalus (see p. 57). This results when the spinal fluid that usually circulates in the brain accumulates and enlarges the head. This fluid creates a lot of pressure on the brain. Hydrocephalus, if it is not treated, may affect the child's intelligence.

Children with spina bifida often require many different kinds of treatment. The young infant with spina bifida usually has surgery to close the opening in the spinal column. When hydrocephalus occurs, a shunt, or drainage tube, is often surgically inserted to drain the fluid from the child's brain to other parts of the body. Children who are paralyzed may need braces, crutches, or a wheelchair to get around. When the child develops back or foot deformities, or other changes, he or she may need surgery to correct them.

Because many children with spina bifida have problems controlling their bowels and bladder, they may need to have surgery to help them. Some children who cannot control when they urinate may learn how to insert a small tube into their bladder to empty it. Some children have surgery so that the bladder or bowel empties into a bag that can be worn next to their skin without being seen.

Although some children with spina bifida may be mentally retarded, most have normal intelligence. Many children learn to get around by walking with braces or crutches, or by using a wheelchair. They may need a lot of help and training to learn toilet skills and become independent. The medical treatment and training that are now available for children with spina bifida will permit many of them to marry and hold jobs when they are adults.

Cleft Lip and Cleft Palate (cleft pál-lat)

A cleft lip was once called a harelip. When a child is born with a cleft lip, the upper lip is split, either on one or both sides of the lip. When a child is born with a cleft palate (the roof of the mouth), there is a groove (called a cleft) that runs along the middle of the roof of the mouth, from the front of the mouth behind the teeth to the back of the mouth. A child may be born with a cleft lip, a cleft palate, or both. These are relatively common birth defects that occur in about one out of every 750 births. If a woman has a child who is born with a cleft lip or palate, she has a 95 percent chance of having a normal child if she becomes pregnant again.

Siblings often wonder what causes cleft lip and palate. Cleft lip and palate are caused by a problem that occurs between the 35th and 37th days of pregnancy. Normally as the cells divide during that time, tissues grow together to form the child's palate and lips. When these tissues do not move in

Cleft lip and cleft palate occur when the tissue that forms the lip and palate does not grow together when the baby is developing inside the mother. Both cleft lip and cleft palate can be corrected by surgery. This is a picture of a child with cleft lip, before and after surgery.

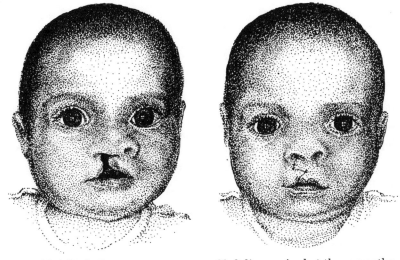

Cleft lip before surgery   Cleft lip repaired at three months

the right direction, there is an opening where the lip or the palate does not grow together. The cause of these birth defects is often not known, although certain drugs and some infections may prevent the tissues from growing together as they should.

Children who are born with cleft lip or palate usually have plastic surgery when they are very young, often before they are two years old. They may have surgery again when they are older to close the cleft and to make it less noticeable.

Some people with cleft lip or palate also have hearing problems. This is because a cleft lip or palate can prevent the middle ear from draining properly. When this happens, the child is more likely to have ear infections. Three out of ten adults born with cleft lip or palate have hearing losses that result from these ear infections. Today, young children with cleft lip or palate may have tiny tubes surgically inserted in their ears to help the ear drain and to prevent infections that might cause a hearing loss.

If your sib has a cleft lip or palate, you may wonder if he will have other problems as well. Cleft lip or palate is an isolated defect—that is, it usually affects only one part of the body. People with a cleft lip or palate are usually not mentally retarded or handicapped in other ways. A person with this birth defect may need the special services of a surgeon, dentist, orthodontist, and speech therapist to correct the defect and to overcome the speech problems that may result. Stacy Keach, the actor, is an example of a person who had a cleft lip and overcame his speech problems to become a talented stage and movie actor.

Tay-Sachs Disease (tay-sacks)

Tay-Sachs is an inherited disease that affects infants and young children. An infant with Tay-Sachs is not able to produce an enzyme—a protein that the body produces—that normally changes a harmful product of the nerve cells into a harmless one. When this enzyme is missing, the toxic substance builds up in the body and causes brain damage and death. Tay-Sachs gets more serious the longer the child has it. A child who is born with the disease usually develops normally for about three to six months. As the harmful product builds up in the brain, the child loses the ability to sit up, babble, and move. The child becomes severely retarded, blind, and deaf. Most children with Tay-Sachs disease die by age five.

Siblings ask us how Tay-Sachs gets passed on if the children who have it do not grow up and have children. Tay-Sachs is a recessive inherited disease. Like other recessive diseases, it is transmitted by carriers—people who have only half the number of the genes needed to produce the disease. A child must receive a gene for Tay-Sachs from *both* parents in order to get the disease. Both parents of the child with Tay-Sachs disease are *carriers*: they each have only one gene for the disease. Neither of them has the disease. If two carriers marry, there is one chance in four that their child will have Tay-Sachs disease, and two chances in four that their child will be a carrier. If a carrier marries a noncarrier, half of their children would be likely to be carriers, and half would not be affected. Remember, these are only predictions, and like the odds on throwing a certain number on a pair of dice, the number of children actually affected in a family may vary from these estimates.

You may wonder if everyone has an equal chance of having a baby with Tay-Sachs. Scientists have traced Tay-Sachs to a genetic change that occurred somewhere in the Jewish population in Eastern Poland in the early 1800s. Before that time, the disease did not exist. Today, the disease is much more common among Jewish people than others. In the non-Jewish population the risk is 1/360,000, but in the Jewish population it is 1/1,600.

Fortunately, people can have a blood test that will tell whether they are carriers of this disease. These screening tests are especially recommended for Jewish people of Eastern European origin, because their risk for the disease is so much higher than the risk for the rest of the population. If a couple has a blood test and find that they are both carriers, they can decide whether they want to risk having a child with Tay-Sachs disease. If only one person is a carrier, the couple will know that none of their children will have the disease, but half of their children are likely to be carriers. Tay-Sachs disease can also be diagnosed by amniocentesis before the child's birth (see p. 52).

Cystic Fibrosis (sis̀-tick fĭ-brō´-sis)

This is a disease that causes the lungs and other organs to produce too much mucus. Our bodies normally produce mucus, a thick fluid, to help us breathe and digest our food. But if there is too much mucus, it interferes with the body's normal functions. Too much mucus may cause bronchitis (an inflammation of the tubes that carry air into and out of the lungs), infections, and lung and heart problems. Children with cystic fibrosis may cough a lot to try to clear their lungs of the extra mucus. In other parts of the body, such as the pancreas, which is an organ that helps us digest food, the mucus blocks the release of substances called enzymes that help us break down food so our bodies can use it.

Siblings ask us if there is a cure for cystic fibrosis. Cystic fibrosis is a chronic disease. This means that a person will have it for life. There is no cure for it, but there are many ways that doctors can treat it to make the person feel better. If cystic fibrosis causes lung problems, the child may take medicine for lung infections, or may inhale medicines to keep the lungs cleared. When the pancreas becomes blocked, the child is not able to get all the necessary nutrients from foods. Vitamins and other nutritional supplements must be taken. Children with cystic fibrosis may have to eat more than normal to get the daily nutrients they need.

A person gets cystic fibrosis when both parents carry the cystic fibrosis gene. If only one parent carries the gene, the child will not have the disease, but will be a carrier for it. If that child marries someone who is also a carrier, there is one chance in four that their baby will have the disease, and two chances in four that the baby will also be a carrier for cystic fibrosis like the parents.

Cystic fibrosis can be diagnosed at birth if a baby has an intestinal blockage. This may be a sign of cystic fibrosis. It may also be detected when the child is older and develops bronchitis or pneumonia. When doctors discover cystic fibrosis early, they can help children lead longer, better, and more normal lives.

Down Syndrome

(This is also called Trisomy 21. In the past, it was called mongolism. It is also sometimes spelled Down's syndrome.)

This condition is named after the doctor who first wrote about it in medical books, Dr. J. Langdon Down. It is the most common known cause of mental retardation that is identified at birth. Over 7,000 children are born each year with Down syndrome. People with Down syndrome used to be called mongols, because they were thought to resemble Asians. This term is no longer used.

A syndrome is a group of signs that are commonly found together in a particular condition. There are over fifty different signs that may lead a doctor to suspect that a baby has Down syndrome. Some of these signs are: floppy muscles, slanted eyes, a single crease across the baby's palm, a nose with a very flat bridge, and very flexible joints. Not all children with Down syndrome will have all of these signs.

If you want to understand what causes Down syndrome, you must know a little about chromosomes. People usually have 46 chromosomes in every cell of their body, except for the male's sperm cells and the female's egg cells, which have 23 chromosomes. Usually, at conception, the 23 chromosomes from the father's sperm cell join with the 23 chromosomes from the mother's egg cell. The fertilized egg, which now contains 46 chromosomes, will divide and grow and eventually become a baby. The chromosomes contain genetic information that is passed on to the baby. For example, if you have your father's eyes and your mother's hair, it is because the chromosomes you inherited from your parents directed your body's cells to grow that way.

Sometimes, for reasons we do not understand, sperm or egg cells divide the wrong way, so that the egg or sperm cells end up with 24 chromosomes instead of 23. At conception, then, one parent's 23 chromosomes will combine with the other parent's 24 chromosomes. The fertilized egg will then have a total of 47 rather than 46 chromosomes. The fertilized egg with 47 chromosomes may divide and grow like any other fertilized egg with one big difference: it will have one extra chromosome. Each of the chromosome pairs have been numbered from 1 to 23 so that they can be studied. The extra chromosome that causes Down syndrome is usually added to the 21st pair. This is why Down syndrome is also called Trisomy (for three) 21. The extra 21st chromosome is responsible for the characteristics seen in children with Down syndrome.

As we said, in most cases Down syndrome results when the sperm or egg cells do not divide properly. In a very few cases (about 4 percent) a child with Down syndrome will inherit the extra chromosome from a parent who does not have Down syndrome but who is a carrier (see p. 70). This is the translocation type of Down syndrome. In these cases the parent only has 45 chromosomes, because part of one of the parent's number 21 chromosomes is added onto another chromosome.

Most of the time, Down syndrome causes some mental retardation. Children with Down syndrome may also have heart and lung problems. They may have hearing and vision problems. Some may have to wear glasses. They may have little tubes inserted into their ears so that fluid does not collect inside their ears and prevent them from hearing.

Siblings sometimes tell us that they have heard that people with Down syndrome don't live very long. They ask us if that means their brother won't live to grow up and be an adult. In the past, many children with Down syndrome did not live long because of their heart and breathing problems. Today, a child with Down syndrome can have open-heart surgery to repair a heart defect. Children with Down syndrome can take medicine to control infections such as pneumonia (new-mō'-nee-ya) that once were the cause of death.

Sibs often ask us about the special programs and classes their baby brother or sister with Down syndrome attends. In the past, people thought that children with Down syndrome would not be able to learn, and parents of children with Down syndrome were often told to put their babies in institutions (see p. 92). Special education programs for babies, called early intervention programs (see p. 86), have helped children with Down syndrome learn far more than anyone would have thought possible twenty years ago. Children with Down syndrome learn many of the things other children learn, but it takes them longer. Everyone in the child's family can share in helping the child learn to walk, talk, and read. When they are older, persons with Down syndrome may learn to work in a restaurant or greenhouse or in a sheltered workshop (see Chapter 8, p. 94). Adults with Down syndrome may live in a group home, where they do most things for themselves but where there are adults who can help them when they need it.

Prader-Willi Syndrome (praý-der wil'-ly)

Like children with other syndromes, children with Prader-Willi syndrome have certain things in common. When they are babies, they have very floppy muscles. This makes it hard for them to suck and swallow milk like most babies. The baby's mother must often spend many hours trying to feed her child. The child's development is often slow. He may not crawl, sit up, walk, talk, or ride a tricycle until much later than other children his age.

By the time the child is about two or three years old, he or she usually begins to have a serious weight problem. This is when parents may first find out that their child has Prader-Willi syndrome. Unless the child is on strict diet, he or she will become very overweight. This can cause serious medical problems when the child grows up. These problems include diabetes, heart disease, and respiratory (breathing) problems.

No one knows for sure what causes Prader-Willi syndrome. Most children with the syndrome have these things in common: they have very floppy muscles; they are very overweight; they are slower to develop skills than other children; their faces are alike in some ways (they often have a triangular-shaped mouth and a narrow face); and they are shorter than other children their age and other members of their family. Many children with this syndrome also have small hands and feet, a curved back, skin problems, and eating problems. About half of all children with Prader-Willi syndrome are mentally retarded. Most children with Prader-Willi who are retarded can learn to read and do simple arithmetic.

Many children with Prader-Willi syndrome can control their weight if they stay on a very low-calorie and low-protein diet. But this is hard for them to do. When they are put on a diet, they may steal food and have temper tantrums if they can't have the food they want. Many families must lock the refrigerator and the cupboards so that the child cannot sneak food between meals. The family can help the child by not giving him food that is not on his diet, and by telling him how happy they are when he stays on his diet. Sometimes the whole family goes on a diet, and keeps no food in the house that the child with Prader-Willi cannot eat. It is important for the family to help the child learn to control how much he eats while he is still young. When he is older and has his own spending money and goes out on his own, the family will not be able to control what he eats. Then the child must be able to use self-control.

It is also important for children with Prader-Willi syndrome to get regular exercise, because this can help them control their weight. Even very young children can get some exercise each day if they ride a tricycle or bicycle. Parents and siblings can help the child with these activities until he is old enough to do them on his own. Older children may jog or do other exercises to control their weight.

As we said, the exact cause of Prader-Willi syndrome is not known. Families who are worried about whether the syndrome is hereditary should see a genetic counselor (see Chapter 8, p. 91). Siblings and parents who would like to learn more about the syndrome or write to other families of children with Prader-Willi syndrome can write to this group:

Prader-Willi Syndrome Association
5515 Malibu Drive
Edina, Minnesota 55436

Chapter 5

Other Causes of Handicaps

In Chapter 4, we learned how some children are born with their handicaps. These handicaps may result from genetic changes that the child inherits or changes that occur after conception as the fertilized egg is developing. Other handicaps are caused by things that happen to the child as he is being born or soon after he is born. Some handicaps can be caused by a lack of air, inherited allergies to certain foods, diseases, injuries, or an environment that does not stimulate a young child.

My mom says that my sister Jenny's handicap was caused because she didn't get enough air when she was born. Aren't some handicaps caused at the time of birth or soon after?

One of the most common causes of handicaps is one that happens to the child at the time of birth.

Anoxia (ăn-oẋ-ee-a)

The prefix "an" means a lack of, and "oxia" means oxygen, the air we breathe. Anoxia usually occurs when an infant does not get enough oxygen during birth. A loss of oxygen is the major cause of infant deaths at birth.

Some cases of cerebral palsy (see p. 73) and mental retardation (see p. 29) may be caused by a lack of oxygen during birth. Fortunately, it seems that most infants who have this problem do not have any permanent effects. But the infant whose brain doesn't have oxygen for a long time may suffer brain damage.

Brain Damage

This term means that part of the brain has been injured. The injury may happen before birth. For example, microcephaly (p. 57) and birth defects (p. 55) may cause brain damage before the infant's birth. Brain damage may also happen during birth as a result of anoxia. Or it may happen after birth as a result of hydrocephalus (p. 57), automobile accidents, or other head injuries. A child who has a disease such as encephalitis (an infection that affects the brain), or meningitis (p. 71), or a very high fever may have brain damage. Brain damage may result in cerebral palsy (p. 73), autism (p. 44), or epilepsy (p. 76). A person who has brain damage may be mentally retarded as a result.

PKU

One inherited food allergy can actually cause mental retardation. It's called PKU. These letters stand for phenylketonuria (fee-nil-kee-tōe-nū´-ree-a). PKU is an inherited condition that can result in mental retardation and other problems. But if PKU is treated in time with a special diet, mental retardation can be prevented.

PKU occurs in about one in 10,000 to 15,000 births and is an autosomal recessive condition. That means that each parent must contribute one abnormal gene in order for the infant to be born with PKU. When a mother and father are both carriers for the PKU gene, each will have only one of the abnormal PKU genes, and neither parent will have PKU. But when the couple has children, each child has a 25 percent chance of being born with PKU—that is, 25 percent of the time the child will receive two abnormal genes that cause PKU, one from each parent. Two-thirds of the parents' normal children will also be carriers for PKU, like their parents.

Children with PKU are born without an enzyme they need to break down an amino acid in the body. Usually, this amino acid is used by the body to help

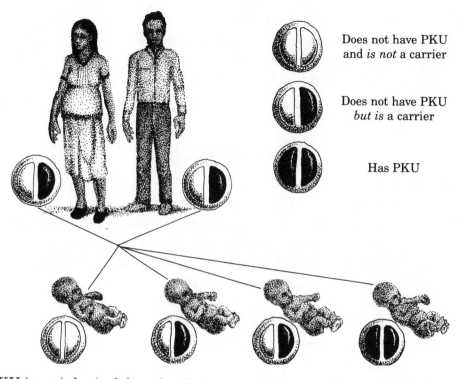

Does not have PKU
and *is not* a carrier

Does not have PKU
but is a carrier

Has PKU

PKU is an inherited disorder that can result in mental retardation if it is not detected and treated. PKU is an autosomal recessive condition, which means that it occurs only when the child receives an abnormal gene from each parent.

bones, muscles, and internal organs grow. When the enzyme is not present, the amino acid is not broken down, and it builds up in the body. Too much of the amino acid can cause mental retardation, behavior disorders, delayed speech, seizures, and muscle problems.

In all states, infants must be tested for PKU shortly after birth. When a blood test shows that the infant has PKU, the child is placed on a special diet. On this diet the child cannot eat foods that are high in protein, such as eggs, milk, cheese, meats, and poultry, but has to eat low-protein foods such as fruits, vegetables, and grains. The child may take a special artificial amino acid mixture, vitamins, or minerals to make sure his diet is complete.

Children may find it harder to stay on this special diet as they get older. They want to eat what their friends eat. Sometimes they get tired of the foods in their diet. Family and friends can help these children stay on the PKU diet by encouraging them.

Siblings often ask us how long their brother or sister must stay on a special diet. We don't know the answer to that question yet. Some studies show that a woman with PKU who is no longer on a special diet and who becomes pregnant may have a retarded child. Women with PKU who wish to have children may need to stay on the diet until they no longer want to have any more children.

Meningitis

One infection that may hurt a young child's brain and cause permanent handicaps is *meningitis* (men-in-jī'-tis). The young child who has meningitis often has a high fever, stiff neck, vomits, has a headache, and may have convulsions, which are violent movements of the arms and legs. A case of meningitis looks much like a serious case of the flu, and it usually affects children under the age of five. Unlike the flu, meningitis may have serious permanent effects. The high fever often leads to brain damage and deafness. Meningitis may also cause hydrocephalus (extra fluid in the brain), paralysis (inability to move part of the body), loss of muscle control, and mental retardation. Meningitis may cause cerebral palsy (see p. 73) or epilepsy (see p. 76) when the infection damages the brain.

Accidents

Other handicaps are caused by injuries the child receives. Some of these injuries may result from accidents. For example, a girl who falls and hits her head may have brain damage and may be mentally retarded as a result of the fall. A child who is in a car accident may injure her legs so that she is paralyzed and cannot walk.

Child Abuse

Child abuse occurs when a parent or another adult mistreats a child. Usually, this term is used to mean that the adult hurt the child physically by hitting or beating the child. Child abuse is often called the "battered child syndrome" because abused children suffer bruises, burns, broken bones, or cuts. Some of these injuries may heal, but others never go away. The greatest dangers of child abuse are that the child may receive permanent brain damage or may die from an injury.

A parent can also do harm without hitting or striking the child. Neglect is a kind of child abuse that happens when an adult does not give the child the things needed for growth and development. The adult may not give the child enough food, medical care, love, or supervision.

Sibs often ask us why adults abuse children. This is a hard question to answer. Social workers and others who work with families of abused children have found that many adults who abuse children were also abused when they were young. Adults who think their child is different from other children are more likely to abuse their child than other parents are. For this reason, handicapped infants and premature infants are "at risk" for child abuse. This does not mean that every handicapped and premature child will be abused; it only means that these children have a higher than normal chance of being abused.

Child abuse has many causes. Certain things about the child, the parent (or adult), and the particular time and place come together to trigger child abuse. Not all grown-ups who abuse children are bad people. Many times the parent who abuses the child is under a lot of stress. The parent may have had a very unhappy childhood. Some parents who abuse their children do not understand how children develop. They may expect too much of their very young child. When the child can't do what's expected, the parents get very angry. If the child is handicapped, the parent may express his or her disappointment or impatience with the child by abusing him.

Doctors, nurses, social workers, and psychologists are people who often work together to help a family in which there is child abuse. Sometimes the abused child will live with a foster family for a while until the parents get help. Often the person who abused the child will go to talk to a counselor or take a class in child development. Other help like daycare, financial aid, or homemaking services may be given to the family to relieve the pressures that may have caused the parent to abuse the child. The goal of everyone who works with the family is to protect the child and to keep the family together. If the abuse does not stop, the child will be taken out of the home and put in a safe foster home.

In most states, doctors and teachers must report suspected cases of child abuse to the local child welfare or child protection agency. If you should ever be aware of child abuse, talk to your teacher so that help for the child, the parents, and the family can be given as soon as possible.

Chapter 6

Neurological Problems: Cerebral Palsy and Epilepsy

Your brain, your spinal cord, and the nerves in your body are all part of your nervous system. Your nervous system helps you control and coordinate your movements. It regulates your body's functions and allows your body to respond to stimulation (heat, cold, pain, different textures, sounds, smells, and tastes). Cerebral palsy and epilepsy are called neurological disorders because they affect how the nervous system works, especially how it controls and coordinates body movements.

Cerebral Palsy

Cerebral palsy, sometimes called CP, is the name given to any muscle disorder that is caused by damage to the brain. "Cerebral" refers to the brain, and "palsy" refers to a lack of muscle control. CP is a developmental disability, which means it affects how a child grows and learns.

Cerebral palsy occurs when there is damage to parts of the brain that control movement. The damage usually occurs before, during, or soon after birth, although the damage may happen any time during the child's development (from birth to eighteen years). The most common cause of cerebral palsy is a lack of oxygen, often at birth. Cerebral palsy may also be caused by accidents, maternal diseases, and infections.

Cerebral palsy is not a disease; you can't catch it. Once the person's brain is damaged, it does not get any worse. There is no "cure" for cerebral palsy; but special equipment, therapy, and training can help a person with cerebral palsy control certain movements and communicate needs.

Other kids at my brother Carl's school also have cerebral palsy. Some are in wheelchairs and some can't talk. Others can walk and talk. Why are they so different?

People who have cerebral palsy are not all the same. Some must use wheelchairs or crutches, while others can walk without help. People with cerebral palsy often have trouble talking. Some may have to use picture boards with special symbols to let people know what they need. Others can speak clearly. Sometimes people with cerebral palsy have vision and hearing problems or are mentally retarded. It is important to remember that many people with cerebral palsy are as smart as anyone else, even though they may be very physically handicapped. One man with cerebral palsy, named Christy Brown, wrote two books (*My Left Foot* and *Down All the Days*) about his life, even though he could move only one toe to type.

Are there different types of cerebral palsy? How do they affect a person?

You may hear someone talk about one of the three main types of cerebral palsy: spastic, athetoid, or ataxic. These words describe the kinds of movements the person with CP makes.

Spastic cerebral palsy makes it hard for a person to move. The person's movements are very stiff because parts of the body do not receive the messages the brain usually sends to make a person move smoothly. The parts of the body that are affected depend on the part of the brain that was injured. *Hemiplegia* (hĕm-ee-pleé-gee-ya) occurs when one side of the brain is injured, causing the opposite side of the body to be paralyzed. For example, if the left side of a child's brain is injured, the right side of the body will be affected. The child will have *right spastic hemiplegia. Quadriplegia* (quad′-ra-plee-gee-ya) oc-

Different types of cerebral palsy

Cerebral palsy is caused by damage to different parts of the brain. Athetoid cerebral palsy is caused by an injury to the basal ganglia, and ataxic cerebral palsy is caused by damage to the cerebellum. A child who has spastic cerebral palsy has damage to the motor cortex or cerebrum. He may have difficulty moving his arms and his legs, depending upon which part of the brain is damaged.

Spastic

Ataxic

Motor cortex

Diplegia

Hemiplegia

Quadriplegia

Cerebellum

Athetoid

Child's legs are most affected

Only one side of the body is affected, the side opposite the side of the brain that is injured

Both arms and legs are affected

Basal ganglia

curs when the part of the brain called the cerebral cortex is severely damaged. The person with quadriplegia has spasticity or stiffness in both arms and both legs. If a person has *spastic diplegia* (die-pleé-gee-ya), the legs are affected more than the rest of the body. When only the person's legs are affected, the condition is called *paraplegia* (par-a-plee-gee-ya).

You may have heard a doctor say that your sib has *athetoid* (ăth′-a-toyd) cerebral palsy. This causes a person to have involuntary and uncontrolled movements. This form of cerebral palsy is different from spastic cerebral

75

palsy. Spasticity is caused by injury to an area of the brain where movement *originates*. Athetoid cerebral palsy is caused by an injury to the part of the brain that *regulates* movement. Persons with athetoid cerebral palsy have muscles that are sometimes stiff and jerky, like those of a person with spastic cerebral palsy, and other times floppy, like those of a child with Down syndrome. Because of these shifts in muscle tone, the person with athetoid CP has special problems eating, speaking, sitting, and standing up.

Another kind of CP, called *ataxic* (ā-tăx̆-ik) cerebral palsy, is caused by damage to the part of the brain called the cerebellum. A person with ataxic cerebral palsy (sometimes called ataxia) may have a very poor sense of balance, and may walk the way a drunk person walks. He may not be able to judge distances, and may reach further than he has to when he tries to grasp an object.

People with cerebral palsy are being helped by advances in education, medicine, and technology to overcome the effects of their conditions. Organizations such as United Cerebral Palsy (UCP) provide support, information, education, and advocacy (speaking out on their behalf) to persons with cerebral palsy and their families. Local UCP centers are found in most cities. To find the one in your area, check your phone book or contact

> United Cerebral Palsy Associations, Inc.
> 66 East 34th Street
> New York, New York 10016

Two forms of therapy that are helpful to people with cerebral palsy are physical therapy and occupational therapy (see p. 86). These kinds of therapy are also used to help children with other handicaps who have trouble moving or using a part of the body, or learning how to take care of themselves.

Epilepsy (ĕp-il-ĕp-see)

Sally, my little sister, has these spells where she just stops, stares, and drools. It looks weird, but it doesn't seem to bother her. My mom says she has epilepsy. I thought people who have epilepsy fall down. Are there different kinds? What causes it?

Epilepsy is a disorder of the central nervous system that causes repeated seizures. A person who has a seizure temporarily loses control over certain parts of the body. Seizures are sometimes incorrectly called spells or fits. Seizures happen to people with many different diseases, but more often to people with epilepsy.

Seizures

Seizures are caused when the brain cells are abnormally active. The brain contains about one hundred billion nerve cells, or neurons. These cells normally send messages to the rest of the body through chemical and electrical signals. When the neurons send too much electrical energy through the parts of the brain that control how we move, feel, or sense things, they cause a seizure. The brain is not damaged when a person has a seizure. After the seizure is over, the brain returns to normal.

Most of the time we do not know why a person has seizures. Sometimes siblings ask us whether something they did caused their brother or sister to have a seizure. You cannot cause a person to have a seizure.

Two types of seizures are absence seizures and tonic-clonic seizures. *Absence seizures* are sometimes called petit mal seizures. *Petit mal* (pĕt-tee mal) is French for "little ailment." A child who has an absence seizure may stare, blink, or twitch and be unaware of people or things around him. These seizures usually last less than ten seconds. The child may not remember having the seizure when it is over. These seizures can be hard to recognize because the child may seem to be daydreaming or just not paying attention.

Most people think of a *tonic-clonic* (or grand mal) seizure when they think of epilepsy. These seizures involve the entire body. Before the seizure actually begins, the person may have an *aura*, a funny feeling that a seizure is about to happen. Next, the person may pass out and fall to the floor. He may have very irregular breathing, and may even stop breathing for a moment. His body will stiffen, his teeth will clench, and his whole body will begin to jerk. He may bite his tongue or lose control of his bladder and wet himself. When the seizure, which usually does not last more than two minutes, is over, the person may feel tired and confused, sometimes for as long as several hours.

Another kind of seizure, called the *partial simple seizure*, begins with a twitching in one part of the body, like the thumb or toe. The seizure gradually spreads to other body parts. During the partial simple seizure, unlike absence and tonic-clonic seizures, the person will usually remain aware of his surroundings. In some cases, the seizure may spread and become a grand mal seizure, and the person may lose consciousness.

A *partial complex seizure* is more common in teenagers and adults than in young children. The person may initially smell, taste, hear, or see things that are not there, and then will appear to be in a daze or a trance. He will make certain movements, like smacking his lips, chewing, or scratching or tugging at his clothes. He may perspire, become pale, salivate (the mouth will produce a lot of saliva), or get very pink. These seizures last only a minute or two, and afterward the person may be confused and may not remember what happened.

First Aid for Seizures

It can be frightening to see someone have a tonic-clonic seizure, because you want to help but may not know how. The most important thing to remember is to try to protect the person from getting hurt while the seizure lasts. The Epilepsy Foundation of America suggests the following first aid during a seizure:

1. Keep calm and reassure other people who may be nearby.
2. Clear the area around the person of anything hard or sharp.
3. Loosen ties, collars, or anything around the person's neck that may make breathing difficult.
4. Put something flat and soft, like a folded jacket, under the head.
5. Turn the person gently on his side. This will help him breathe more easily. Do *not* try to force his mouth open. It is *not* true that a person having a seizure can swallow his tongue, and you can injure the person's teeth or jaw by trying to hold his tongue down.
6. Don't hold the person down or try and stop his movements.
7. Stay with the person until the seizure ends.
8. Be friendly and reassuring when the person becomes conscious again.

Causes

Epilepsy, the condition that causes seizures, has many different causes. Head injuries, birth defects, poisons, brain tumors, anoxia (see p. 68), and

78

certain infections (see "Meningitis," p. 71) may damage the brain's electrical system and cause epilepsy. In about half of the cases, the cause is unknown. Some families have a history of epilepsy. If a parent has epilepsy, his or her child has a greater chance of developing epilepsy than a child of nonepileptic parents, but the child is still much more likely not to have it.

Treatment

Treatment of epilepsy varies. Most often, epilepsy is controlled with a medicine or combination of medicines. Often the doctor must try out several different medicines to find the kind and amount that will control the seizures. Sometimes this medicine will have side effects. A side effect is an effect that medicine has in addition to controlling the epilepsy. The amount of medicine the child will take has to be changed as he grows. Children with epilepsy that is being controlled with medicine can do just about everything that children without epilepsy can do. Of the people whose seizures are treated with medicine, about half will have their seizures completely controlled, and 30 percent will have fewer seizures. For about 20 percent, the medicine will not help the seizures. Sometimes a special diet can prevent seizures that result from vitamin deficiencies. In rare cases, surgery can help people with partial complex seizures.

Epilepsy is often diagnosed in children with cerebral palsy, Down syndrome (see p. 64), or mental retardation. Most people who have epilepsy have normal intelligence and lead normal lives. Famous people in history who have had epilepsy include James Madison and Thomas Jefferson, early American presidents. Neil Young, the rock star, has epilepsy and has talked about it in interviews.

If you or your family would like to have more information about epilepsy you should write to:

Epilepsy Foundation of America
4351 Garden City Drive
Landover, Maryland 20785

Chapter 7

Education and Services for Children with Handicaps and Their Families

My mom and dad go to these meetings at my brother's school with other parents who have kids with problems like my brother's. They say they learn about special programs and laws for handicapped people. What special programs are there for handicapped people? Why do they need special laws?

Many children with handicaps will need some kind of special education and special services when they are growing up. This kind of assistance will help the children make the most of their abilities. A law that was passed in 1975 makes it possible for all children with handicaps to get the training they need in school programs that best meet their needs.

In some parts of the country, the families of children with handicaps can get help to care for their child. Respite care, which we describe in this chapter, gives the family a break by providing someone to care for the child who understands the child's special needs.

Special education and respite care are services that children with special needs receive when they are growing up. After they turn twenty-one, some children with handicaps will continue to benefit from special living and work settings. We describe some of these services and programs in Chapter 8.

The school, work, and living programs and placements we describe are designed to help the person with special needs learn and do as much as possible for himself. Yet many people with handicaps are prevented from becoming as independent as possible by something called handicapism.

Handicapism

You may know about other "isms"—like racism, which is the unfair treatment of someone because of that person's race, or sexism, which is the unfair treatment of someone on the account of that person's sex. Handicapism results from stereotypes of what a person with disabilities can and cannot do. A stereotype is a very simple and unfair idea of what a member of a certain group is like. For example, a stereotype of a person with handicaps is often that the person cannot do very many things for himself or herself. Siblings of people with handicaps know that this is too simple a way of looking at people with handicaps. You know that your sibling's abilities differ even from those of other children with the same handicap. A person with a handicap is the victim of handicapism when someone sees only what the person who is handicapped *cannot* do instead of what the person *can* do. Handicapism can prevent people with disabilities from getting jobs that they are able to do.

Thanks to laws that have been passed, employers are encouraged to hire people with handicaps. A law that was passed in 1975 and which is described below helps children with special needs get the kind of education that will prepare them to become as independent as possible.

PL 94-142: The Education for All Handicapped Children Act

In 1975, Congress passed a law that requires that all children— handicapped or not—receive a free and appropriate education. This means that the states must let children with special needs go to public schools for free and get the special help they need. The law says that states must offer special education for children with the following handicaps: mental retardation, deafness and hearing impairments, speech impairments, blindness and visual impairments, serious emotional problems, orthopedic handicaps, other health impairments, deafness and blindness, learning disabilities, and multiple handicaps. This federal law, PL 94-142, says that children with these handicaps who are between the ages of three and twenty-one must get special education services unless the state law differs from the federal law. In many states, the laws do not say that children between three and five and between seventeen and twenty-one must receive special education. Therefore, in those states, only children between six and seventeen receive special education.

The Education for All Handicapped Children Act says that children with special needs must receive related services as well as special education. These other services include free transportation to school, occupational therapy, speech therapy, special tests, and certain services for their parents, such as counseling. The law says that children with handicaps must receive these services in the least restrictive environment (LRE). This means that whenever possible, children with handicaps must be included in classes with nonhandicapped children. Some children with severe handicaps may only attend classes with nonhandicapped children for part of the day. Other children with mild handicaps may take most of their classes with nonhandicapped children. A child with a mild handicap may go to a resource room to work with a teacher or group of handicapped children for only part of the day.

This law requires that each child with a handicap have an Individualized Educational Program (IEP). This is a plan that the child's teacher and parents work on together. The IEP describes what the child can do at the beginning of the school year, what goals the child will work on during the year, the special kinds of help the child will get to meet those goals, and how the child will be tested at the end of the year.

States can get money from the federal government to offer these special programs if the states do certain things. Each state must conduct a search to find the handicapped children who need special education. Then the state must plan how those children will be served. States that do these things can then get more money from the federal government to pay for the special education programs they will offer for the handicapped children they find.

The Individualized Educational Program (IEP)

An IEP is a plan that is usually written at the beginning of the school year. It lets parents and school staff know what the handicapped child will be working on during that school year. Every child with a handicap must have his or her own IEP, and it must be updated every school year. The IEP clearly

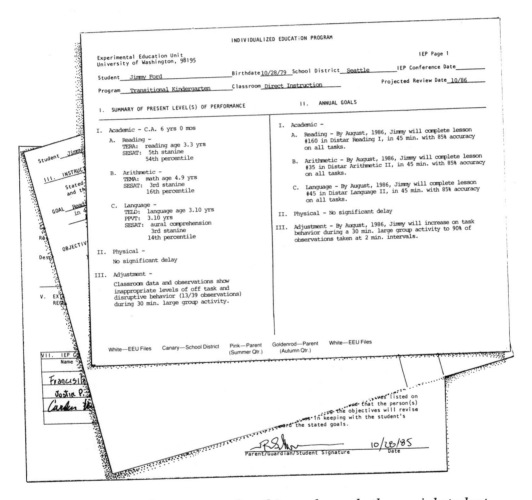

The IEP describes among other things, the goals the special student will work on during the year.

states in writing the goals the child's school will be helping the child to meet that year.

The IEP is written at a meeting of the child's teacher, parents, and others in the school who will be working with the child. All these people will have something to say about what goes into the child's IEP. At the meeting, which is usually held early in the school year, they will go over the results of tests taken by the child. They will use the information in the tests to help decide what the child should learn during the coming school year. Sometimes the child will need special services to help meet those goals. For example, a child may need physical therapy or speech therapy. The IEP will say whether the child will stay in the regular classroom or go to a resource room or a special classroom to get these services. The IEP will also list the dates when the child will get these services.

Children with special needs can go to school and get the extra help they need thanks to PL 94-142. There are many schoolbooks, games, tests, and even computer programs that are made just for children with handicaps. These school programs and materials help each child learn as much as he can in his own special way.

Physical Therapy

I know that kids with CP need to go to physical therapy and occupational therapy, but I don't know what they do there. What is the difference between PT and OT? Do they hurt?

If your sibling has difficulty sitting up, crawling, walking, or moving in other ways, he or she may receive physical therapy (PT) at a hospital, clinic, school, or at home. A physical therapist (sometimes called a PT) is someone who is trained to test how muscles move and how strong they are. These tests help the physical therapist plan physical therapy activities for the child. For example, if an infant cannot lift its head, the physical therapist may use a toy to encourage the child to raise its head. If the child's arms or legs do not move as they are supposed to, the therapist may move them the way they should move. The PT may stretch the arm or apply pressure to the leg to help it move right. Therapists teach parents how to do these things at home, so that the

A physical therapist helps children who are slow to develop certain skills, or who need to overcome the effects of a physical handicap.

child will get lots of practice learning these movements. If a child needs braces, crutches, or a wheelchair, the physical therapist will help the child learn to use them properly. Besides cerebral palsy, children with Down syndrome, juvenile arthritis, or neural tube defects often need physical therapy to learn to move properly, to develop their muscles, or to unlearn reflexes (automatic movements) that interfere with normal movements. Physical therapists also help people who have had accidents or have lost the use of part of their body.

Siblings have asked us whether physical therapy hurts. Sometimes the exercises the physical therapist does with a child do hurt a little. This is because for physical therapy to work best, the child's muscles have to stretch. When the child practices the exercises and stretches the muscles, the exercises won't hurt.

Occupational Therapy

An occupational therapist (sometimes called an OT or a developmental therapist) is someone who can help a child who has difficulty eating, dressing, bathing, playing, or using the toilet. By testing a child's ability to do many of the things you do every day, the occupational therapist finds out what the child can and cannot do. The OT chooses activities and exercises that will help the child play and care for himself or herself with less help. Unlike the physical therapist, who is most interested in the child's overall muscle tone and strength, posture, and ability to move, the OT helps a child learn to do specific things. For example, an OT may work with a child at a clinic, school, hospital, or in the home to help that child learn to move his arm to his mouth so that he can feed himself.

Early Infant Intervention Programs

If you have a baby brother or sister who has a handicap, or if your parents think that there is some reason your baby sibling may not be learning to do things other babies the same age can do, then your baby sib may need to go to an early intervention program. These programs or schools for babies are sometimes called infant education programs, or stimulation programs, or early education programs. They are for babies who are just a few months old to about three years old.

Babies in school? What can a baby learn in school?

You may not have thought that babies could go to school. People used to think that babies couldn't do very much, let alone learn things. In fact, not so long ago, many people thought that babies could not even see or hear very well. But ever since psychologists (people who study how people, including babies, learn and act) and other researchers have studied babies, they have helped us understand that babies are pretty smart, and are learning all the time. Babies can see and hear quite well when they are born. They practice using their eyes when they play with their parents. They learn to connect sounds they hear with things, like bells or rattles, that they see making noises. They learn how to use their hands to reach for things they see and hear, like a bottle, or rattle, or a sister's ponytail. Most of the things babies learn, they learn when they are playing. That way, learning happens all the time as the baby grows.

If babies learn by playing, why do they have to go to school?

When a baby has a handicap, he or she is not always able to learn the same things that a nonhandicapped baby learns just by playing. For example, Judy,

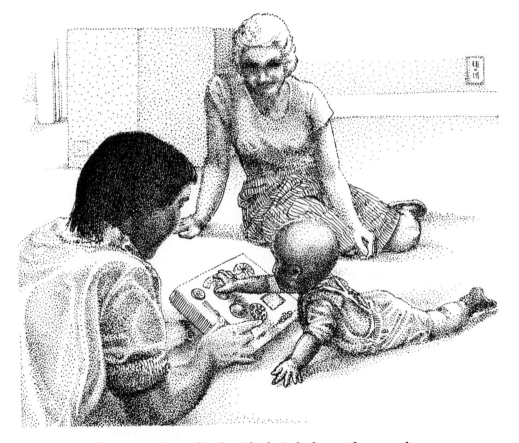

Parents go to school with their baby so they can learn how to help their baby learn at home.

a nonhandicapped baby, began to learn how to crawl when she saw a toy that she liked at the other end of the room. She would also try to crawl when her mother stretched out her arms and called to Judy to crawl over to her for a big hug. A baby who cannot see or hear well, or who is blind, will not be able to see or hear those things that made Judy want to crawl. This is when an early intervention program can help a baby with a special problem. If the baby cannot see, the teacher in the program can help the baby listen to sounds that will interest it and make it want to find out more about them. The teacher can help the baby move its arms and legs to crawl over to a music box, or to a ball with bells inside.

Infant programs are different from kindergarten or first grade. Most of the time the baby's mother or father goes to school with the baby. Parents go to school with their baby so they can learn how to help it learn at home. This is really important, because babies are home most of the time, and they learn mostly by playing with their parents. In the infant program, parents learn games and exercises that they can play with their baby to help the baby sit up, roll over, walk, or drink out of a cup. Parents will be able to do these things with their baby when they go home. They can also teach others in the family how to help the baby when they are playing, feeding, or dressing it.

Respite Care

It's really hard for our family to do things together. My brother's behavior problems make it hard for us to take him anywhere. They also make it hard to find a baby-sitter for him. My parents say they are trying to get some "respite care" for Sam. What's respite care?

A respite (rĕsś-pit) is a rest. Respite care gives the family a break from caring for a handicapped child. This rest may be very short—maybe just a few hours, long enough for the parents to go out to dinner or a movie. It may be longer, like a week or two, to let the whole family take a vacation together without the handicapped child. During this respite, a person who knows about the special needs of the handicapped child will take care of the child so that the family does not need to worry. This person may be specially trained or may have had experience in caring for a family member who is handicapped.

Respite care gives a family some time off from caring for their special child.

All families need some times when they can relax together. This can be very hard to plan when there is a child who has many special needs. If a child is severely handicapped, someone must always be looking after the child, and the family never can do things together. Families may not be able to hire a neighborhood baby-sitter to look after the child with a handicap, because the sitter would not know how to take care of the child's special needs. As a result, parents may never get to go to a movie together, and families may have to give up vacations. The parents and other children in the family may miss out on the times together that help families feel close.

This is why respite care is so important. It can prevent families from getting "burnt out" from caring for the handicapped child. It can help them feel close. This helps them all work together to take care of the child with special needs. The sad news is that respite care is sometimes hard to find. In many cities, parents cannot find someone they trust to care for their handicapped child. Or if trained respite care is available, it is often very expensive. Some states have respite care programs. These states pay people to give respite care to families with handicapped children. We think that families should be able to get respite care when they need it—both in emergencies and when the family needs to take a break and go away together.

If you want to find out if you can get respite care in your community, call your local Association for Retarded Citizens. It should be listed in the telephone book. Someone there will be able to tell you if there are people who offer respite care in your area. If there aren't, you may want to ask them what it would take to start a respite care program in your town. In some cities, groups like the Camp Fire Girls or Boys, or groups of retired people, offer respite care for families.

Chapter 8

The Future

Thinking about the future can make you feel both excited and worried. It can be exciting to daydream about growing up, having an interesting job, independence, and a family. On the other hand, thinking about finding a job, and earning enough money to buy all your own food and a house—that can be pretty scary. You may ask yourself a lot of questions when you think about the future, like "How many children will I have?" "How much money will I make?" "What will I be?" Brothers and sisters of children with special needs also think about the future, but they may also have a few questions that other siblings *don't* have. They may wonder:

—What's going to happen to my sibling with special needs when she grows up?

—Will I have to take care of my sib when my parents get older or die?

—Will I have a baby with a handicap like my brother's?

For many sibs these are tough questions that are hard to talk about with their parents. The answers will depend on your sib's handicap, your family's beliefs, and your community's resources. Here are some ideas to help you get the answers that will match your needs.

When Sibs with Handicaps Grow Up

What will happen when my sib grows up?

Just as you will someday grow up and move out of your parents' house, it is normal to expect that your brother or sister will someday live away from home. Where your sib will live and what he or she will do during the day will depend on your sib's handicap and the resources available in your community. Sometimes people with handicaps continue to live at home when they grow up. But this can be harder for parents as they grow older, especially if the handicapped person can't do much for himself.

Many adults with handicaps live in group homes. Some of these homes have programs so the handicapped adults can go to work during the day. Some states have more of these programs than other states. Some are better than others. You can find out what programs your state has from the local Association for Retarded Citizens (ARC). To get the address of the ARC in your state, check your phone book, contact the United Way, or write:

> National Association for Retarded Citizens
> P.O. Box 6109
> 2709 Avenue E East
> Arlington, Texas 76011

It's important to remember that your sibling will not necessarily live or work in the same place all her life. Just like you, she may learn skills so she can move to a new home or job. She will always be able to take advantage of new living or job opportunities that may come up in the future. Here are some programs that your state may have for adults with handicaps.

State Institutions

In some states, institutions are the only places besides nursing homes or hospitals for adults with severe handicaps. In the past, many institutions have provided very poor care and little stimulation for residents. Some state institutions are getting better, but many still do not treat handicapped persons well. In some institutions, handicapped persons do not receive any training to help them learn as much as they are able to learn. Some of the buildings are very old. They often do not have modern equipment. A big problem is that all state institutions separate the people who live there from the rest of the people in the community. Some states are closing their state institutions and finding better ways to care for severely handicapped citizens. These institutions are often replaced by group homes. In other states, people who live in state institutions and who have severe handicaps are learning vocational skills. A person with these skills may then be able to find a place in a group home and a sheltered job in the community.

Group Homes

Many states have group homes for handicapped people. States that close their institutions often transfer their residents to group homes. These are often cheerful, small houses or apartments. They are often located in neighborhoods that are near the handicapped person's family and community services, like a pool or park and shopping center. Many are furnished with modern equipment. Trained staff are on hand to help meet the residents' many health and care needs. People who live in group homes are often required to go to school, to a job training program, or to hold a job. People in group homes often have jobs around the home, like cleaning their room or helping cook dinner. They are encouraged to participate in community activities.

Foster Homes

Some states provide foster homes for handicapped children and adults. People who run foster care homes are paid and licensed by the state. The state gives someone a license to have a foster home if that person shows he or she can give good care to someone who is handicapped. These are individuals who understand and can take care of the special needs of adults with handicaps.

Supervised Independent Living

Adults with mild handicaps have more living skills and need less help and supervision than more handicapped adults. Because of this, they may be able to live on their own, or with a little outside help, in an apartment, boarding house, co-op, YMCA, YWCA, or condominium. These adults often have jobs and can do most things for themselves. Someone who is paid by the state may come in sometimes to help with paying bills, cleaning, or to be sure the person is eating properly.

Jobs and Daytime Activities

Whether you sib works during the day, attends a day activity center, or stays at home will depend on your sibling's handicap and the local programs that are available. In some communities, there are day activity centers for adults with moderate, severe, or many handicaps. At these centers, adults have a chance to learn and practice their skills, have fun, and get out and meet people. They practice language skills, self-care skills, and enjoy planned recreation like swimming or sports. Although most adults with severe or many handicaps will not be able to work, there are more and more training programs that take advantage of their abilities.

Sheltered Workshops

These are set up in many communities for adults with moderate and mild handicaps, although more workshops are beginning to recognize that adults with severe handicaps can also learn vocational skills. Sheltered workshops take orders from businesses and do jobs for them. The kind of job a person does in a sheltered workshop depends on the person's abilities. The person may stuff envelopes, sort hardware, put together an electronic circuit board, bake bread, or use tools to build furniture. People who work in sheltered workshops get paid for their work. They have opportunities to make friends during their lunch breaks and after work.

94

Many handicapped adults may have a good chance of getting a job in the community. This also depends on their abilities, what jobs there are in the community, and how well employers understand the abilities of handicapped people. If the person is mildly retarded, he may be able to get a job clearing tables or washing dishes in a restaurant or school. He may be a janitor or a groundskeeper, or may help assemble parts of appliances. People who are not mentally retarded, but who have handicaps like cerebral palsy, or vision or hearing impairments, are able to do regular jobs in their community if they have proper training and if employers are willing to hire them.

Caring for a Grown-up Sibling

Will I have to take care of my special sibling when my parents are no longer around?

The answer to this tough question is very simple: you will have only those responsibilities you want. There are state programs and agencies that will take care of your sib. Their staff are trained to make decisions for him when needed. Many people, however, want to make sure that their sib lives in the best possible place, and enjoys a good daytime program and enough of the little "pluses" that make life enjoyable. They want to have a say in the lives of their brothers and sisters.

There are legal ways to make sure that you can have a voice in your sib's life when you grow up, if that is what you want. You will need to talk to your parents about your part in your sibling's future. It is *their* responsibility to make sure that your brother or sister will be cared for when they are no longer around. Ask your parents if they have any plans for your sibling's future. If they haven't, let them know that you are thinking about this, and show them this book. Some families set up wills or trusts for their handicapped children. These are ways of setting aside money for their special child's future. When some siblings grow up, they decide they want to become the legal guardian for their handicapped brother or sister. A legal guardian makes important decisions for another person. You must go to court to become a legal guardian. Your local Association for Retarded Citizens can give you and your family more information about how to plan for your special sib's future.

"What will happen when my sib grows up?
Will I have to take care of him when my parents are no longer around?"

Worries about Your Own Future

Will I have a baby with a handicap like my sibling's?

The answer to this question depends on the type of handicap your sibling has. If the handicap is a result of an accident during or after birth, you have as good a chance as anyone of having a healthy baby. If your sibling was born with a handicap, there is a chance that his handicapping condition can be passed on to your children. *Your chances depend on the handicap.* Doctors we talked to say that if you are unsure if your sib's handicap is hereditary, you should ask your parents and perhaps contact a genetics clinic and ask them.

96

Genetics clinics are often located at state university medical schools and at large hospitals. A phone call to your doctor or to a nearby hospital can help you find a genetics clinic in your area. Also, you can write to one to these three places to find out where your nearest genetics clinic is:

March of Dimes
1275 Mamaroneck Avenue
White Plains, New York 10605

National Genetics Foundation
555 West 57th Street
Room 1240
New York, New York 10019

National Clearinghouse for
Human Genetic Diseases
1776 East Jefferson Street
Rockville, Maryland 20852

It is important that you and your brothers and sisters understand your chances of having children with a hereditary handicap. This is information your parents can help you obtain, or that your doctor, school nurse, or counselor can help you find out about.

Conclusion

It was hard to stop writing this book. There are so many questions we wanted to answer for siblings: questions about different kinds of mental retardation; questions about handicaps that are much less common than the ones we included, but that some siblings might want to know about; questions about special medical treatments for particular problems.

We realized that we couldn't include everything in this book, or it would be so long that you wouldn't want to read it. Instead of trying to answer every question, we only tried to give you simple, direct, and up-to-date answers to the most common questions siblings asked us. For example, we wrote about mental retardation because many children who have less common handicaps are also mentally retarded. We wrote about cerebral palsy and epilepsy because they are more common than other handicaps that also affect the brain and the nerves. We wrote about PL 94-142 because that law affects more handicapped children than many other laws that were written to help only certain groups of handicapped children.

And even though we limited the subjects we covered, we still could not include all the information you may want to know about a particular handicap. That is why we have included in the Appendix the names and addresses of organizations you can write to for more information. For example, if your brother is deaf, you may want to write to one of the groups we have listed for more information about sign language or special programs for deaf people. Or you may write to the United Cerebral Palsy Association for more information about a particular kind of cerebral palsy.

We hope we have been successful at what we set out to do: help sibs realize that other children with special brothers and sisters have similar feelings and worries, and help sibs understand more about handicaps. But we won't know for sure how well this book works unless you tell us. That is why we have included a page that we would like you to fill out and return to us. We want you to tell us how you liked the book, and how we could make it better. We would like it very much if you would take a few minutes to answer the questions on the last page and let us know if this book helped you understand your feelings and your sibling's handicap. You don't need to fill in your name and address unless you want to, or unless you want to ask us a question. If you found this book in the library, don't rip the page out. Ask the librarian to help you make a photocopy of the page, or just write out the questions and answers on another sheet of paper. We're more interested in your thoughts than the type of paper you write them on. We've enjoyed writing this book. We hope it's helped you make sense of feelings and experiences in your life that are sometimes hard to understand.

Appendix

Books about Handicaps for Young Readers

Autism

The Devil Hole by Eleanor Spence. Lothrop, Lee and Shepard, 1977.
The October Child by Eleanor Spence. Oxford University Press, 1976.
Please Don't Say Hello by Phyllis Gold. Human Sciences Press, 1976.

Blindness and Visual Handicaps

Belonging by Deborah Kent. Ace Books, 1979.
Listen for the Singing by Jean Little. E. P. Dutton, 1977.
Being Blind by Rebecca Marcus. Hastings House, 1981.
Tom and Bear by Richard McPhee. Thomas Y. Crowell, 1981.
Laurie by Diane Greig and Alan Brightman. Scholastic's Feeling Free, 1978.
Connie's New Eyes by Bernard Wolf. Harper and Row, 1976.
Sally Can't See by Palle Petersen. John Day Company, 1977.
Spectacles by Ellen Raskin. Connecticut Printers, Inc., 1968.
The Seeing Summer by J. Eyerly. J. B. Lippincott, 1981.

Cerebral Palsy

Let the Balloon Go by Ivan Southall. Methuen, 1968.
Mine for Keeps by Jean Little. Little, Brown and Company, 1962.
Howie Helps Himself by J. Fassler. Albert Whitman and Company, 1975.

Deafness and Hearing Problems

Silent Dancer by Bruce Hlibok. Messner, 1981.
Apple is My Sign by Mary Riskind. Houghton Mifflin, 1982.
The Swing by Emily Hanlon, Bradbury. 1979; Dell, 1981.
A Show of Hands by Mary Beth Sullivan and Linda Bourke. Addison-Wesley, 1980.
A Button in Her Ear by A. Litchfield. Albert Whitman and Company, 1976.
I Have a Sister, My Sister is Deaf by Jeanne Whitehouse Peterson. Harper and Row, 1977.
Lisa and Her Soundless World by Edna Levine. Human Sciences Press, 1974.
Claire and Emma by Diana Peter. Adam and Charles Black, 1976.

Emotional and Behavioral Handicaps

Walkie-Talkie by Phyllis Green. Addison-Wesley, 1978.
Mad Martin by Patricia Windsor. Harper and Row, 1976.

Epilepsy

Epilepsy by Alvin and Virginia Silverstein. J. B. Lippincott Junior Books, 1975.
A Handful of Stars by Barbara Girion. Charles Scribner's Sons, 1981.
What if They Knew? by Patricia Hermes. Harcourt Brace Jovanovich, 1980.

Language Problems

Trouble With Explosives by Sally Kelley. Bradbury, 1976.
I Can't Talk Like You by Althea. Dinosaur Publications, 1982.

Physical Handicaps

Ginny edited by Alan Brightman and Kim Storey. Scholastic's Feeling Free, 1978.
Hollis edited by Alan Brightman and Kim Storey. Scholastic's Feeling Free, 1978.
Hackett McGee by Charles Grealish and Mary Jane Grealish. Scholastic's Feeling Free, 1978.
Alesia by Eloise Greenfield and Alesia Revis. Philomel, 1981.
Wheelchair Champions by Harriet May Savitz. Harper and Row, 1978.
Sports for the Handicapped by Anne Allen. Walker, 1981.
Run, Don't Walk by Harriet May Savitz. Accent Special Publications, 1979.
Physical Disabilities by Gilda Berger. Franklin Watts, 1979.
Mister O'Brien by Prudence Andrew. Heinemann, 1972.
Mark's Wheelchair Adventures by Camilla Jessell. Methuen, 1975.

Spina Bifida

Janet at School by Paul White. Adam and Charles Black, 1978.

Learning Disabilities

Keep Stompin' Till the Music Stops by Stella Pevsner. Seabury, 1977.
But I'm Ready to Go by Louise Albert. Bradbury, 1976.
Kelly's Creek by Doris Buchanan Smith. Harper and Row, 1975.
My Brother Barry by Bill Gillham. Andre Deutsch, 1981.
'I Own the Racecourse!' by Patricia Wrightson. Hutchinson, 1972.

Mental Retardation

Welcome Home, Jellybean by Marlene Shyer. Granada, 1981.

The Alfred Summer by Jan Slepian. Macmillan, 1980.

He's My Brother by Joe Lasker. Albert Whitman and Company, 1974.

My Brother Steven is Retarded by Harriet Sobol. Macmillan, 1977.

A Look at Mental Retardation by Rebecca Anders. Lerner Publications, Minneapolis, Minnesota, 1976.

Don't Take Teddy by Babbis Friis-Baastad. Charles Scribner's Sons, 1967.

The Summer of the Swans by Betsy Byars. Viking Press, 1970.

A Racecourse for Andy by Patricia Wrightson. Harcourt, Brace, and World, 1968.

Take Wing by Jean Little. Little, Brown, and Company, 1968.

Mary Fran and Mo by Maureen Lynch. St. Martin's Press, 1979.

My Sister by Karen Hirsch. Carol Rhoda Books, Minneapolis, 1977.

A Special Kind of Sister by Lucia Smith. Holt, Rinehart, and Winston, 1977.

She's My Sister by Jane Claypool Miner. Pitman Learning, Inc., Belmont, California, 1982.

The Blue Rose by G. Klein. Lawrence Hall and Company, 1974.

A Place for Everyone by Tana Reiff. Fearon-Pitman, 1979.

Sticks and Stones by Lynn Hall. Follett, 1972.

Between Friends by Sheila Garrigue. Bradbury, 1978.

It's Too Late for Sorry by Emily Hanlon. Bradbury, 1978.

Don't Forget Tom by Hanne Larson. Thomas Y. Crowell, 1978.

A Little Time by Anne Norris Baldwin. Viking Press, 1978.

The Hayburners by Gene Smith. Dell, 1975.

General Books about Handicaps

Friends by Melva Jackson Edrington. Instructional Development Corp., P.O. Box 361, Monmouth, Oregon, 97361, 1978.

Like Me by Alan Brightman. Little, Brown and Company, 1976.

What If You Couldn't . . . .? A Book About Special Needs by Janet Kamlen. Charles Scribner's Sons, 1979.

Who Will Take Care of Me? by Patricia Hermes. Harcourt Brace Jovanovich, 1983.

The Raft by Alison Morgan. Abelard-Schuman, 1974.

What Do You Do When Your Wheelchair Gets a Flat Tire edited by D. Biklen and M. Sokoloff. Scholastic Book Services, 1978.

Like It Is: Facts and Feelings About Handicaps From Kids Who Know by Barbara Adams. Walker, 1979.

Winners: Eight Special Young People by Dorothy Siegel. Messner, 1978.

Feeling Free by Mary Beth Sullivan, Alan Brightman, and Joseph Blatt. Addison-Wesley, 1979.

About Handicaps: An Open Family Book for Parents and Children Together by Sara Bonnett Stein. Walker, 1984.

Health, Illness and Disability: A Guide to Books for Children and Young Adults by Pat Azarnoff. R. R. Bowker, 1983.

Resources on Specific Handicaps

Autism

National Society for Autistic Children
1234 Massachusetts Avenue, N.W.
Suite 1017
Washington, D.C. 20005

Blindness

American Council for the Blind
1211 Connecticut Avenue, N.W.
Washington, D.C. 20006

American Foundation for the Blind, Inc.
15 West 16th Street
New York, New York 10011

National Association for Visually Handicapped
305 E. 24th St., #17C
New York, New York 10010

Cerebral Palsy

United Cerebral Palsy
    Association, Inc.
66 East 34th Street
New York, New York 10016

Cystic Fibrosis

Cystic Fibrosis Foundation
6000 Executive Boulevard, Suite 309
Rockville, Maryland 20852

Deafness

National Association of the Deaf
814 Thayer Avenue
Silver Springs, Maryland 20910

Alexander Graham Bell Association
3417 Volta Place
Washington, D.C. 20007

Down Syndrome

Down Syndrome Congress
706 South Bunn Street
Bloomington, Illinois 61701

Epilepsy

Epilepsy Foundation of America
4351 Garden City Drive
Landover, Maryland 20785

Genetic Diseases

National Clearinghouse
  for Human Genetic Diseases
1776 East Jefferson Street
Rockville, Maryland 20852

National Foundation
  for Jewish Genetic Diseases
609 Fifth Avenue
Suite 1200
New York, New York 10017

National Genetics Foundation, Inc.
555 West 57th Street
Room 1240
New York, New York 10019

National Foundation/March of Dimes
1275 Mamaroneck Avenue
White Plains, New York 10605

Learning Disabilities

Association for Children
  with Learning Disabilities
4156 Library Road
Pittsburgh, Pennsylvania 15234

The Orton Society
8415 Bellona Lane
Towson, Maryland 21204

Mental Retardation

National Association
  for Retarded Citizens (ARC)
2709 Avenue E East
P.O. Box 6109
Arlington, Texas 76011

Prader-Willi Syndrome

Prader-Willi Syndrome Association
5515 Malibu Drive
Edina, Minnesota 55436

Spina Bifida

Spina Bifida Association of America
343 South Dearborn Street
Room 317
Chicago, Illinois 60604

Tay-Sachs Disease

National Tay-Sachs
  and Allied Diseases Association
122 East 42nd Street
New York, New York 10068

Source of General Information on Handicaps

National Information Center for Handicapped Children and Youth
1555 Wilson Boulevard
Rosslyn, Virginia 22209

Groups for Siblings

Siblings Helping Persons with Autism through Resources and Energy (SHARE)
National Society for Children and Adults with Autism
Suite 1017
1234 Massachusetts Avenue, N.W.
Washington, D.C. 20005
(publishes scrapbook for and by siblings, holds meetings for parents and siblings, publishes newsletter for and about siblings, sponsors poster contest)

Sibling Information Network
Department of Educational Psychology
Box U-64
The University of Connecticut
Storrs, Connecticut 06268
(publishes newsletter for and about siblings which features articles written by siblings)

Siblings Understanding Needs (SUN)
Department of Pediatrics C-19
University of Texas Medical Branch
Galveston, Texas 77550
(publishes newspaper written by
siblings)

Siblings for Significant Change
823 United Nations Plaza, Rm 808
New York, New York 10017
(provides information for families,
refers siblings to events and
services of interest)

Youth Advocates for Retarded Citizens
5522 University Avenue
Madison, Wisconsin
(608) 231-3335

Index

Sibling Feedback Form

Siblings: Please use this page to tell us how you liked this book. (Don't write on this page if this is a library book. Copy your answers on another sheet of paper.)

Dear Don, Patricia, and Rebecca:

I really liked these parts of your book:

But I still don't understand these things that you wrote about:

I think that you should also have written about:

If I were writing a book for sibs, I would:

I would like you to help me answer these questions *(please be sure to include your name and address if you want us to write to you)*:

My Name

Address

Age

My sibling's handicap

I found this book in: (bookstore, library, school)

   Is there anything else you would like to tell us about our book or about being a special sib?

Return this form to:
The Sibling Handbook Project
Experimental Education Unit   WJ–10
Child Development and Mental Retardation Center
University of Washington
Seattle, WA 98195